THE IMMORTAL ACADEMIC

Surviving and Thriving in Academia provides short, accessible books for navigating the many challenges, responsibilities and opportunities of academic careers. The series is particularly dedicated to supporting the professional journeys of early and mid-career academics and doctoral students, but will present books of use to scholars at all stages in their careers. Books within the series draw on real-life examples from international scholars, offering practical advice and a supportive and encouraging tone throughout.

Series Editor: Marian Mahat, The University of Melbourne, Australia

In this series:

Achieving Academic Promotion
Edited by Marian Mahat, The University of Melbourne & Jennifer Tatebe, University of Auckland

Getting the Most Out of Your Doctorate: The Importance of Supervision, Networking and Becoming a Global Academic
Edited by Mollie Dollinger, La Trobe University, Australia

Coaching and Mentoring for Academic Development
By Kay Guccione & Steve Hutchinson

Women Thriving in Academia
Edited by Marian Mahat, The University of Melbourne, Australia

Academic Resilience: Personal stories and lessons learnt from the COVID-19 experience
Edited by Marian Mahat, Joanne Blannin, Elizer Jay de los Reyes, & Caroline Cohrssen

Academic Mobility and International Academics: Challenges and Opportunities

By Jasvir Kaur Nachatar Singh, La Trobe University, Australia

The Impactful Academic is a must-read for the academic community. It effortlessly demystifies impact, bringing together a range of expert voices whose collective experience covers everything from planning pathways through to demonstrating effects. The book is full of actionable advice from those working within the research sector, reflecting the realities of 'doing impact' in a range of settings and within differing national agendas. *The Impactful Academic* will steer any reader in the right direction as they embark on impact for the first time or are looking to strengthen their existing practice.

–Dr Julie Bayley, Director of Research Impact Development & the Lincoln Impact Literacy Institute, University of Lincoln, UK

Written in an accessible and colloquial style, *The Impactful Academic* is a how-to guide for academics with the courage to step out of their comfort zone and dip their toe into the impact world to demonstrate the benefits of the work they do. Authors lure the reader into a reflective impact state of mind while providing actionable tips on how to immerse themselves in impactful scholarship. For those keen to become more impactful, this book will prepare you for the journey. Essential reading for early career academics and those seeking faculty promotion.

–Dr Melanie Barwick, PhD, CPsych Senior Scientist, SickKids Research Institute Professor, Psychiatry, Faculty of Medicine, University of Toronto

The *Impactful Academic* is a comprehensive guide that includes everything an academic needs to achieve impact from their research. It contains invaluable practical advice that is both evidence-based and accessible, drawing on experience from around the world. This is an essential guide to impact for early career and senior researchers alike.

–Mark Reed, Professor and Centre Director, Scotland's Rural College (SRUC), and CEO of Fast Track Impact

The Impactful Academic provides practical strategies for success in a contemporary landscape that values societal impact. This book is a valuable resource for those in the early stages of their academic careers, for senior scholars embarking on new projects with community partners, and for university staff and administrators who support impact work. The book's focus on self-assessment and reflection, including tips and techniques from experts working in various disciplinary contexts, means there is something here for everyone. By covering such topics as community engagement strategies, research translation practices, and ways to track evidence of impact, this book serves as a go-to guide for academics to foster social change and make a difference in the world.

–Prof Lisa M. Given, Director, Social Change Enabling Capability Platform and Professor of Information Sciences at RMIT University in Melbourne, Australia

THE IMPACTFUL ACADEMIC

Building a Research Career That Makes a Difference

EDITED BY

WADE KELLY
Monash University, Australia

United Kingdom – North America – Japan – India
Malaysia – China

Emerald Publishing Limited
Howard House, Wagon Lane, Bingley BD16 1WA, UK

First edition 2022

Reprints and permissions service
Contact: permissions@emeraldinsight.com

British Library Cataloguing in Publication Data
A catalogue record for this book is available from the British Library

ISBN: 978-1-80117-845-7 (Print)
ISBN: 978-1-80117-842-6 (Online)
ISBN: 978-1-80117-844-0 (Epub)

Printed and bound by CPI Group (UK) Ltd, Croydon, CR0 4YY

ISOQAR certified
Management System,
awarded to Emerald
for adherence to
Environmental
standard
ISO 14001:2004.

Certificate Number 1985
ISO 14001

INVESTOR IN PEOPLE

To the academics who choose to make a difference and the community members who welcome them in.

CONTENTS

PREFACE

The impact of research is being discussed more and more in higher education – both from the project-based level to how universities are judged to contribute to the broader community through their research efforts. Understanding what impact means and articulating how research produces an impact beyond the generation of new knowledge is becoming a crucial component of the academic landscape. But how ready are we for this? What does impact mean, and how can this be demonstrated? The concept of impact may not be entirely new, but its centrality in the research agenda is. The increasing use of impact in grant applications, institutional strategies, and national assessment schemes means researchers and institutional administrators need to become more 'impact literate' and build impact into their planning and assessing research activities.

During my career as a biomedical researcher, and now in a research administration role, I have seen impact increase in prominence. Looking back, I can see where my research has had impact but I also recognize that the work did not always have impact built into the design. Over the last decade, I have engaged more with stakeholders, which has helped focus the research conducted in my laboratory and also diversify our funding streams from traditional funding sources to ones that include partnering for impact. In my current research administration role, impact is front and centre – it is even in my position title! As the research landscape changes, we need to adapt and move with this change. *The Impactful Academic* is a very useful resource that bridges this impact knowledge gap, with practical and accessible approaches. Many of these approaches were not available to me during my research training (back when the internet as we know it now was still new) but I can see now how important engagement and impact skills are for my students and colleagues to possess.

The Impactful Academic is a timely contribution to the discussion of research impact and provides a rich spectrum of contributions from academics and professional staff across the globe that will guide researchers in developing themselves into impactful academics.

The book is split into nine chapters. The first introduces the topic of impact and provides an overview of how the book can be used. Chapters on navigating impact within an academic institution follow, with tips on identifying support and expertise to guide the researcher's journey to impact. Early on, the book sets a vibrant tone, with activities and exercises included to guide the reader in developing their impact story. The book cleverly unravels the different levels of impact from the researcher level through the institution and community including identifying and engaging with stakeholders. *The Impactful Academic* provides a reflective opportunity for the reader to assess their progress on their impact pathway and learn from others. Rounding off the book is a chapter that describes an impactful academic and advice for keeping on track with impact with the development of impact goals and plans that need regular attention.

The book is written with a broad readership in mind which is helped by the multidisciplinarity and expertise of the authors. The content is very accessible, and the chapters make for thoughtful reading. The exercises throughout this book provide an opportunity to put the book down and reflect, and they offer practical steps to increase one's profile and guide their impact journey.

The Impactful Academic is suitable for academics at all levels as well as professional staff working in the research space. Of course, while more junior academics might benefit more in the long run by developing their impact journey earlier, more established scholars and research leaders will similarly benefit by following the practical advice in the book and embedding impact in the research agenda of their organisation.

Wade Kelly has brought together a group of authors who have produced an excellent resource that will have an impact in developing researchers and supporting their impact journeys.

Professor Andrew Hill
BSc(HONS) DIC PhD (Imperial)
Deputy Vice-Chancellor Research & Impact,
Victoria University, Melbourne, Australia

ACKNOWLEDGEMENTS

I wish to thank the chapter authors. In the early days of assembling this book, conversations with them formed the shape the book needed to take. We are better together. Their contributions extend beyond insightful chapters. I thank them for their time, intelligence, and support, but more than anything, I thank them for their passion. The people who have contributed to this book make universities and communities better.

Thank you to the series editor, Marian Mahat. Marian offered encouragement throughout and graciously understood delays due to moves, new jobs, and a global pandemic. Thanks as well to Joann Cattlin for introducing us. You're a connector extraordinaire.

Kim Chadwick is the exact person you dream will work for a publisher. Kim, thank you for calming me by figuratively holding my hand throughout this process and for being an absolute delight.

Thank you to my husband Phil for always supporting me and the projects I take on when I already have said yes to too many things. For the multitude of ways you deserve to be thanked, I would need another book.

Finally, my thanks to all the academics I have worked with over the years who have taught me so much. Sometimes I get lost in the bureaucracy – forms, deadlines, assessments, and spreadsheets. All it takes to remind me why I love what I do is to hear about someone's research and the ways they are helping to transform conditions for individuals, industries, and communities. We need more of you.

ABOUT THE CONTRIBUTORS

Dr Lauren Albrecht is an educator and a researcher, who likes to explore the spaces where these two fields intersect, including strategic communication, partnership building, knowledge mobilisation and evidence-informed decision-making. Lauren works in faculty development, academic and strategic consulting, and community-oriented research.

Richard Hayman, MA, MLIS, is an Associate Professor and Digital Initiatives Librarian at Mount Royal University (Calgary, Canada). He is a researcher-practitioner with interests that include open access and scholarly communications, educational technologies and evidence-based practice in academic library settings.

Michael Johnny has managed the Knowledge Mobilization at York University (Toronto, Canada) since 2006. As a university-based service professional, Michael makes connections for collaboration with researchers, students, policy professionals, community organisations, entrepreneurs and industry leaders. He operates to maximise the social, economic and environmental impacts of research for public good.

Lucy Jowett is Research Impact Manager at Northumbria University (UK) where her expertise, enthusiasm and commitment to impact-rich research culture contributed to an outstanding result for Northumbria in the 2021 research assessment. She contributes thought leadership and supports networking on research impact nationally and internationally.

Dr Wade Kelly is Director, Research Excellence and Impact at Monash University (Melbourne, Australia). Wade works at the nexus of engagement and impact, providing strategic advice to university leadership, faculties and institutes to embed impact into university culture. He is a sought-after speaker and commentator on impact in higher education.

Dr Caroline Osborne is a consultant, academic and IAP2 practitioner specialising in research, engagement and evaluation, using engagement to design impactful policy and strategy. Caroline is an Adjunct Fellow at USC and has published in international journals on transformational community engagement, impact measurement, social capital and city futures.

Alisha Peart is Research Impact Manager at Northumbria University (UK). Alisha is an experienced programme manager, grant development manager and now a research impact specialist. Alisha has jointly led the transformative change in the research impact culture at Northumbria University, culminating in the outstanding success for Northumbria in the 2021 Research Excellence Framework assessment.

Dr David Phipps is the administrative lead for all research programmes and their impacts at York University (Toronto, Canada). In addition to other awards, he received the Queen Elizabeth II Diamond Jubilee Medal for his work in knowledge mobilisation. He sits on knowledge mobilisation committees around the world and is Network Director for Research Impact Canada.

Dr Anneliese Poetz is Senior Program Manager, Knowledge Mobilization (for Social Innovation) at Brain Canada. Anneliese combines her previous role at Capitalize for Kids implementing solutions for child and youth mental health agencies with experience working with researchers to maximize impact of research for prevention, diagnosis, treatment and cure of brain disorders.

Dr Cathie Scott is committed to supporting people and organisations to achieve their potential through executive coaching, research and evaluation, and strategic facilitation. She has supported strategic design, collaboration, knowledge mobilisation and evidence-informed decision-making in health-care practice settings and as a senior executive in health and social service organisations.

Dr Erika E. Smith is an Associate Professor and Faculty Development Consultant at Mount Royal University (Calgary, Canada). Her research interests include social media and digital literacies, educational development and learning technologies in higher education.

Dr Faith Welch is Research Impact Manager at Waipapa Taumata Rau – University of Auckland (New Zealand). Faith is passionate about growing impact literacy and mobilising a positive impact culture within Australasia. She has launched several initiatives to facilitate connection, collaboration and the sharing of best practice related to impact development.

Dr Rebekah (Becky) Willson is an Assistant Professor at the School of Information Studies at McGill University (Montréal, Canada). Dr Willson's research is in information science, focusing on the information people need and how they find, share and use that information, particularly during times of transition and uncertainty.

1

IMPACT PRIMER: THE WHAT, WHY AND HOW OF IMPACT

Wade Kelly

ABSTRACT

Impact has generated much discussion in higher educa-tion in recent years, and it is not abating. This chapter lays the groundwork to build an understanding of what impact is, where it has come from and where it is likely to be going in higher education. The various roles of uni-versities and academics and the value of knowledge generation and dissemination to communities outside of academia are explored. Understanding impact and how it is enacted, monitored, evaluated and reported is essential to position impact within one's academic practice. While various definitions of impact have been adopted in different contexts, the focus is on leveraging those defi-nitions as an academic. The language of impact is important as it determines how some disciplines are privileged and others potentially are disadvantaged. The chapter encourages academics in the latter category of disciplines to be active in helping shape the conversation around impact in their contexts. The final section discusses where impact may be going within higher education, how to get the most out of the book as a researcher and what each chapter contributes to becoming an impactful researcher. There is no one right way to be an academic; the reader is encouraged to use each chapter to help hone and refine their academic trajectory given their own epistemological beliefs.

Keywords: Research impact; early career research; REF; research engagement; higher education; professional development; academia; career development; tenure; promotion; PhD student

Impact has generated much discussion in higher education in recent years, and it is not abating. This chapter lays the groundwork to build an understanding of what impact is, where it has come from and where it is likely to be going in higher education. The various roles of universities and academics and the value of knowledge generation and dissemination to communities outside of academia are explored. Understanding impact and how it is enacted, monitored, evaluated and reported is essential to position impact within one's academic practice. While various definitions of impact have been adopted in different contexts, the focus is on leveraging those definitions as an academic. The language of impact is important as it determines how some disciplines are privileged and others potentially are disadvantaged. The chapter encourages academics in the latter category of disciplines to be active in helping shape the conversation around impact in their contexts. The final section discusses where impact may be going within higher education, how to get the most out of the book as a researcher and what each chapter contributes to becoming an impactful researcher. There is no one right way to be an academic; the reader is encouraged to use each chapter to help hone and refine their academic trajectory given their own epistemological beliefs.

In recent years, the momentum of impact in higher education has been building. Spurred on by national assessments of research impact, it is now present in many facets of academic life. Depending on your institution and location, you may be asked to account for impact in multiple places and at various times, including grants, research plans and annual reports. This chapter traces some of the threads that have resulted in increased prominence of impact in higher education and highlights the various skills the impactful academic will need as impact becomes increasingly integrated into academic life and the higher education landscape.

I work closely with academics across career stages daily. Many are thinking about impact for the first time; some have been doing impactful work for years – often without calling it impact – and some are world-leading researchers who have a deep abiding passion for generating an impact through their research.

Through dozens of consultations over many years, I have found that people are often myopically focused on the research project at hand and are rarely asked to zoom out and look at the view from the hot air balloon – the view of where they have been, where they are going and where they want to land. While busy chasing grants, the focus can be taken off the big picture. Too often, impact is only seen within the context of a single grant. It is clear for reviewers when the researcher has left their impact statement until the end and attempted to shoehorn impact into their proposed project. Where you have been, where you are going and the impacts you envisage along the way are vital for you to know, as it will strengthen your granting success and increase your project impacts.

I ask a few challenging but straightforward questions of researchers, 'at the end of your career, what would you like your contribution to be' and 'how does this project contribute to your impact goals.' Similarly, in workshops, I encourage participants to think about their career goals – for example, make professor by 40 – but also their career impact goals and how the two intersect. The responses I get are often profound. People have told me that such conversations have changed their career direction and aspirations. Some have said that they had never been asked these questions throughout their many years of schooling.

Whatever stage you are at, it is not too late to ask these questions. This book will help you work through some of the finer aspects of exactly how to enact your impact goals to be an impactful academic, not only within the context of a research project or program but as a fundamental part of how you operate as an impactful academic.

WHERE DID IMPACT COME FROM?

Before we get too deep into the impact conversation, let's talk about what impact is and where it has come from. The term 'impact' has been around for many years, but its meaning began to coalesce around the UK's REF (Research Excellence Framework) exercise in 2014. The REF was the first national assessment of research impact and asked universities across the country to provide case studies of research that demonstrated impact based on their definition: 'an effect on, change or benefit to the economy, society, culture, public policy or services, health, the environment or quality of life, beyond academia' (https://impact.ref.ac.uk/casestudies/FAQ.aspx).

The REF puts a focus on impact in a big way. Academics were not ready for impact; universities were not prepared for impact. In the intervening years, the impact conversation has picked up steam. In preparation for REF 2021, universities in the UK adjusted policies and provided additional resourcing. In the UK, it is particularly prudent to do so as there is considerable funding attached to the results of the REF exercise. Impact matters when it comes down to dollars and cents.

In 2018, the Australian Research Council (ARC) ran the Engagement and Impact (EI) assessment. In Australia, the definition of impact adopted was 'the contribution that research makes to the economy, society, environment or culture, beyond the contribution to academic research' (ARC EI 2018 Framework). All universities participated in this assessment across all disciplines. Once again, institutions and individuals were essentially not prepared to prove how their research made a difference beyond scholarly contributions with quantitative and qualitative evidence.

Furnishing an h-index is easy; providing evidence that your research is being adopted and applied in widespread practice is much more challenging. Academics were generally not building impact into their research plans, and methods to generate evidence of impact had not been widely adopted. While no direct funding was attached to EI, the assessment signalled a change in priorities. No longer was knowledge for knowledge's sake sufficient; the government wanted tangible evidence of the difference research makes in communities, industries, non-profits, health systems and government.

In addition to the REF in the UK and EI in Australia, there are various national, regional and disciplinary research impact assessments around the world (Adam et al., 2018). While the details of each assessment are too specific for this book, it is worth noting that they exist and are flourishing as they have shaped, and will continue to shape, higher education in years to come.

In Canada, academics often provide knowledge translation or mobilisation plans in funding proposals. In the US, funders may ask for broader impacts. While the focus in the process may be different in different jurisdictions – that is, the engagement activities intended to increase adoption and use versus the impact generated because of those activities – the endpoint, the goal, is ultimately to generate an impact. Put simply, impact is not going anywhere.

Much has been written about the definitions of impact and what they include, exclude or marginalise (e.g. Smith et al., 2020). The nuances of how impact is conceptualised make for worthwhile debate amongst policymakers and higher education scholars. However for most academics, what's important is how impact will affect their scholarly practice now and throughout their career – that is, this book's focus. When the hot air balloon lands years from now, will you have driven it to a place you're happy with?

In many ways, impact is still emerging as universities slowly modify policies, implement training and provide resourcing. For aspiring impactful academics, this can be seen as an opportunity. While impact literacy (Bayley & Phipps, 2019) is often relatively low, those who can skill-up their impact literacy and practice are at an advantage in an increasingly competitive academic job market.

BUT WHAT IS IMPACT?

Let's put aside the definitions from funding agencies and governments for a moment. At its simplest, I like to describe impact as the change out there in the world that your research can help generate. Impact is all about change. Change of practice, policy, health outcomes, or how much money is generated or saved. Impact is about positive change for whomever your stakeholders are.

Deciding what impact means to you in the context of your research is essential. Ensuring that it aligns with the definitions employed by the granting agency you are applying for is prudent, but those definitions are likely to morph, change and evolve. Knowing what impact looks like to you and working within the context of an external definition is a good starting place.

Much of the impact conversation centres on grants and other types of funding. The REF, EI and other assessments have shone a light on impact. In response, funders increasingly require applicants to account for the impact they are proposing to generate (prospective impact) or an example of impact they have generated in the past (retrospective impact).

While changes in higher education are often glacially slow, the impact dominos are falling on all aspects of academic life. Impact is increasingly integrated into hiring practices, promotions and annual reviews. Engagement and impact awards (and the various names they go by) at universities, within faculties and schools, and in disciplinary associations are becoming commonplace. It is worth mentioning that these changes have their detractors and supporters and, while impact is not yet ubiquitous, it is gaining a foothold in academic culture.

A FEW WORDS ON STAKEHOLDERS

We tend to get bogged down in language. Various disciplines and regions will use different phrases to describe similar things. I work with multiple disciplines and find *stakeholders* a flexible catchall. So, I'll use it here. For some researchers, it might be end-user, next user or consumer. It might be a partner, collaborator or patient, for others. The label you give to the people or groups you engage with is not paramount; your relationship with your stakeholders is what matters. Ideally, it is a relationship based on mutual respect, equity, trust and shared goals. This is something I discuss in more depth in the final chapter.

I often ask researchers, 'have you asked your stakeholders what their impact goals would be for this project?' or 'from your stakeholder's perspectives, what would be a useful output from the project that they could use?' The number of times they have not asked such questions far outstrips the number of times they have. These simple questions are at the heart of an impactful practice and thinking like an impactful academic. Not focusing only on research publications that will arise but how the research might be adopted and used by partners and beyond.

IMPACT AS OPPORTUNITY

At the heart of this book is the philosophy to move beyond the idea that impact is a means to an end. Knowing how to generate impact and being an impactful academic is not as simple as developing a persuasive impact statement (as Alisha and Lucy discuss in Chapter 4). Being an impactful academic is at the core of your philosophical beliefs about generating new knowledge and the importance of that knowledge being adopted and applied.

In workshops, there is always a contingent of people who want to be told the five steps to 'do impact'. They want to know the silver bullet to ensure that they get that grant and continue building their track record. The difficulty is that the silver bullet does not exist. There is no simple solution to building impact into your project plan. Two researchers in the same discipline researching the same phenomenon using identical methods might have completely different impacts. The impacts and their impact planning should be based on their needs, stakeholder needs, where they want their research findings to go and how people will find and use them.

If I tell workshop participants on day one that impact isn't something that you do, it's something that you live; I lose them. But I'm telling you the reader that now. The academics who truly do impact well, live impact. It is not a slapdash affectation responding to some trend in academia. It is who they are. It is in the conversations they have with their academic partners, the community/industry partners, their funders and their mothers. The impactful academic doesn't have to write an impact statement for people to know their impact, but they are certainly well be prepared to do so.

GETTING THE MOST OUT OF THE IMPACTFUL ACADEMIC

I have drawn on academics and professional staff who support impact to contribute chapters in this book. They come from different disciplines and different areas of the world. What they have in common, however, is their approach to impact. They share similar philosophies about the importance of research, stakeholder engagement, research mobilisation and impact. I firmly believe that impact is a team sport, and their chapters build on this notion.

We start inside the university for Chapter 2 with Rebekah Willson exploring how to identify and leverage collegial and institutional supports for impact. Her research discusses the importance of drawing on supports that exist but are often not readily apparent inside the university. These supports, people and resources, will help you on your impact journey.

Erika Smith and Richard Hayman then take us beyond the physical and virtual walls of the university in Chapter 3 and provide strategies for building an academic profile to build connections and foster community. This is vitally important for the impactful academic. Creating the conditions for people to find you and your work can be daunting, but the authors provide salient strategies for making the most of your time for the most significant results.

In Chapter 4, Lucy Jowett and Alisha Peart encourage the reader to pack their bags for an impact journey. Drawing on countless hours delivering workshops and working closely with academics across disciplines, their approach will prepare you for achieving granting success with impact at the fore.

Caroline Osborne then takes us into the community setting in Chapter 5, where she discusses best practices for stakeholder engagement. The chapter highlights the complementary skills needed to do high-quality engagement work that will lead to impacts. The impactful academic does not need to possess every skill; they need to know what skills are required and draw on the skills and abilities of others when there are gaps.

As the impactful academic does embedded research with stakeholders, results emerge. In Chapter 6, Lauren Albrecht and Catherine (Cathie) Scott help readers navigate a pathway to impact through knowledge mobilisation. Their system ensures that the research outputs meet the needs of stakeholders.

Doing the research, working with stakeholders and mobilising knowledge is only part of the picture. Funders, governments and administration want proof that impact has been generated. In Chapter 7, David Phipps, Anneliese Poetz and Michael Johnny provide a novel approach for collecting and communicating the evidence of impacts. As is the case with all chapters, the approach presented is not limited to a single project but are a set of principles that can be used across the career span.

One of the benefits of the workshop environment is that participants can learn from the experiences of others across career stages and disciplines. Drawing on that learning model, in Chapter 8, Faith Welch presents the experiences of impactful academics to help bring your impact journey to life. This chapter is best consumed slowly with a pen, paper and openness to self-reflexivity.

In the final chapter, the pieces are put together to envision what an impactful academic might look like and, more importantly, what it might look like for you. In the busy life of an academic, it's hard to keep the impact wheels in motion when, so often, there are other persistent pressures. Strategies are discussed to ensure that impact stays on track and in focus.

CONCLUSION

The book is structured so that each chapter builds on the previous one. When I give workshops, I tell participants that they will come away with something useful, transformative even, if they do the work. The approach of this book is similar. There are questions posed to the reader throughout, and if you have the time or inclination to work through them, you will get much more out of the book. If you are early in your career, perhaps pursuing a PhD, I hope this book will provide a little inspiration. Higher education is changing; there is a place in the academy for the impactful academic.

REFERENCES

Adam, P., Ovseiko, P. V., Grant, J., Graham, K. E. A., Boukhris, O. F., Dowd, A.-M., Balling, G. V., Christensen, R. N., Pollitt, A., Taylor, M., Sued, O., Hinrichs-Krapels, S., Solans-Domènech, M., & Chorzempa, H. (2018). ISRIA statement: Ten-point guidelines for an effective process of research impact assessment. *Health Research Policy and Systems*, *16*(1), 8. https://doi.org/10.1186/s12961-018-0281-5

Australian Government, Australian Research Council. (2018). EI (engagement & impact) 2018 framework. Australia.

Bayley, J., & Phipps, D. (2019). Extending the concept of research impact literacy: Levels of literacy, institutional role and ethical considerations. *Emerald Open Research*, *1*, 14. https://doi.org/10.12688/emeraldopenres.13140.1

Smith, K. E., Bandola-Gill, J., Meer, N., Stewart, E., & Watermeyer, R. (2020). *The impact agenda: Controversies, consequences and challenges*. Policy Press.

2

IDENTIFYING AND LEVERAGING COLLEGIAL AND INSTITUTIONAL SUPPORTS FOR IMPACT

Rebekah (Becky) Willson

ABSTRACT

This chapter discusses practical ways that we as researchers can identify and make use of supports that will help further our research impact and advocates for making plans to include impact work from the beginning and taking advantage of opportunities and resources available. The chapter begins by encouraging you to identify your own values related to research impact and to articulate what impact you would like their research to have in the world. This ensures that impact work does not become a tick-box exercise but a meaningful, planned part of their research practice. The chapter then looks at supports – collegial and institutional – from the perspective of information science. The discussion of collegial supports makes the case that colleagues are key sources of practical information, assistance and mentorship; these connections can become information relationships and important parts of your professional network. The discussion of institutional supports makes the case that the landscape of impact can be scattered, so it is important to actively seek out information to help understand the impact environment where you are. Each discussion is accompanied with practical suggestions about how to make the most of opportunities and get the supports needed. The chapter ends with a section aimed at those who are in leadership positions to discuss what can be done to help reduce barriers and provide supports for those who are undertaking research impact projects, including helping to share information and resources about research impact, as well as acting as a mentor.

Keywords: Collegial support; professional networks; institutional support; actively identifying resources; professional values; preparation and planning

For many researchers, our research findings are discussed within our own academic and disciplinary networks. For most of us, this is how we were trained, and these are the spaces we are most comfortable in. With increasing calls to demonstrate impact beyond academia coming from funding bodies and government agencies, a shift is required in planning for, carrying out and disseminating research. Often there seems to be a steep learning curve and few resources available for this work. However, more supports may exist than are readily apparent. With some information and guidance about how to use those resources, much can be accomplished.

This chapter comes from my own work in the field of information science, where I focus on what information people need, as well as how they find, use, share and create information they require. It focuses on what individuals can do to make the most of the resources that are at hand to help undertake impact work. It starts with questions to ask yourself about the type of work that you want to pursue, followed by a discussion of collegial supports (focusing on developing professional networks) and then institutional supports (focusing on understanding the context in which you are working). Finally, there is a discussion about professional development within the area of impact, thinking about the future.

IDENTIFYING YOUR OWN VALUES

Especially when impact work is being driven by funding bodies, it is easy to start thinking in instrumentalist ways – a box to tick on a funding application or annual report. It can also be tempting to contort our work to try to make it into impact work – which can lead to poor research with little to no impact. However, with careful planning, communities can be profoundly affected by your research; this is extremely rewarding for community members as well as for yourself. If you take some time to think about where your interests lie and what really matters to you as a researcher (and as a person), this can help to guide you towards where your energy is best placed. I firmly believe that when our work matches our values, we do better work.

Related to what you value is the way(s) you want to have an impact. It is important to think about how you see your research changing the world around you. For me personally, I want to make academia a better place. In particular, I want PhD students and early career researchers to be better prepared for academic jobs and academic departments to be better equipped to help them in their work. This stems from my values of inclusion and being informed (as a researcher in information science, it will not be surprising that this is a value for me). These values became solidified for me during my first professional job; I felt completely lost and did not know how to find the information I needed to carry out my work. As a result, this became the focus of my PhD research (Willson, 2016). I now do talks aimed at informing PhD students and early career researchers about the experience of finishing off a PhD and transitioning into academic positions, including what to expect and how to prepare yourself (and your CV) for what's next. While this engagement work is within academia, it is aimed at those who will (hopefully) make practical use of my findings. Research engagement and impact work can take place anywhere – and be extremely satisfying.

When you are thinking about your values and your work, some guiding questions to ask yourself are: What is most important about my work? What do I want to change in the world? What do I want to be known for? Where do I already have connections? Who should hear about my work? (See Chapter 1 and 8 for more discussion about identifying your own values.) These questions will hopefully guide you to think about both what matters to you and also what opportunities are available. It is important to consider your own professional goals but to also balance that with openness to what is available. Keeping an eye on funding calls, government priorities, current public interest and your own personal networks can provide you more opportunities to promote the work you care about. In the next two sections, I will discuss collegial and institutional supports to help you in your engagement and impact work.

COLLEGIAL SUPPORTS

We know that colleagues are a key source of information and support for academics (e.g. Miller, 2015; Willson, 2018). What is important – particularly when learning a new skill or working in a new institution – is to build professional networks and 'information relationships' (Cross & Sproull, 2004). Information relationships are connections built between colleagues that facilitate information sharing and contribute to actionable knowledge (e.g. chatting at the photocopier with a colleague who mentions an upcoming internal grant opportunity). These relationships are typically a combination of social and professional connections. This does not mean approaching relationships in a mercenary fashion, but it is useful to recognise that making connections are key to obtaining information and support in our jobs. Additionally, information relationships are not one-sided, with one person providing all the information and support. Each person has a lot to offer; though when starting out on an engagement and impact journey, we may be the main recipient of information and help. However, as we gain expertise, the balance between recipient and contributor shifts.

What You Need

Building professional networks is fundamental, as we know that colleagues can offer mentorship, moral support and practical support, as well as acting as key sources of information. While formal education, training and resources are important sources of learning (such as this book, of course), people are key sources of information and support, particularly when exploring a new topic. (More will be said about professional development at the end of the chapter.) Often, we don't know what we don't know. It can be challenging to understand the role and scope of engagement and impact, as well as to conceptualise what it looks like in our own field.

Governments, funding bodies and university policies can tell us idealised versions of impact, but colleagues can tell us what it's like on the ground – generally more quickly and easily than wading through policy documents. Of course, formal policies are important to understand for contextual purposes, but are often better to fill in blanks or guide specific implementation, rather than introduce us to the field.

What is also important to keep in mind is that colleagues are speaking from their own perspectives, and it is beneficial to talk to many different people with different expertise and experiences. It is also useful to think about the many places where you can develop your professional networks, including your department, university, or academic discipline/ association. Talking to a variety of colleagues can help to navigate not only what successful impact others have achieved and their pathways to generate impact, but also what you would like to reproduce or adapt as part of your own impact trajectory. We need to develop networks of colleagues so that we know who to go to for the type of information, help and support we need.

HOW TO DO IT

Making the Most of Opportunities

Some people naturally enjoy networking and do it well and regularly. Others (like me) have had to build skills in this area. But whatever your natural inclination or skill level, you can do things that will help your networking.

Of course, one way to network is to actively seek people out – identify people you want to talk to and then approach them in person or over email. This can be very effective but, for me, strikes terror into my heart. One of the best pieces of advice I got was to think about networking wherever you are.

Essentially, it's identifying where you can make connections and where information is (or can be) shared. This is reminiscent of the concept *information grounds* from information science, which is a place in which identifiable social groups congregate and will interact; the social interactions that take place will lead to sharing of information (which may or may not be the purpose of meeting) (Fisher, 2005).

You can think of a meeting room at a conference or the lunchroom in your department; there are possibilities to network wherever you meet people and in much more natural ways than gladhanding at a conference reception. This allows you to take advantage of the opportunities you have to meet and talk to your colleagues – conferences and workshops, but also committee meetings, compulsory training sessions, university events, hallway conversations, etc.

It can be tempting to skip department events or to turn up to a committee meeting right at the appointed time. However, whenever colleagues are together, this can be an opportunity to network and find out about what they are doing. Showing up to a committee meeting a few minutes early allows for this. It can also mean getting two things out of every event or meeting – the content of the event as well as a new connection.

Making Connections

Once you've identified where you can network, the next thing is to actually make those connections. One of the best things you can do is to introduce yourself and ask people about their work – academics love to talk about what they do. At worst, you will find out something interesting about someone's research; at best, you will have a new person in your network who can be a resource (a potential information relationship).

It is completely fine to put it out there that you are interested in learning more about impact – and even that you are seeking help and/or mentorship. When people know what you are looking for, they can also direct you to information or other people to talk to, even if they can't help you themselves.

Once you have started to build your network, you may want to consider more strategic networking. This could be seeking specific people out and approaching them. But if directly approaching people is not for you, another way to be strategic is to think again about information grounds and where you could place yourself in the path of the people you are interested in meeting. Seek out impact training or conferences and talk to people at coffee breaks. As a low-risk first step, figure out who at your institution you would like to meet and see if there is an event where this could happen, or be bold and introduce yourself via email.

Of course, meeting people is just the first step. The same principles of cultivating and maintaining relationships apply to information relationships and strategic networking. Keeping in touch is important, as is reciprocity and building rapport. Once you've met someone (or seen them speak at an event), it's great to follow up with an email to thank them for what they've shared. I still use business cards to exchange contact information or look up their university profiles in order to continue contact (refer to use of LinkedIn and other social networking in Chapter 3).

Offering to buy someone coffee can be a great way to further a conversation, as well as to get to know them better. It's also great to contact them with brief updates about your engagement and impact work to let them know how their help or mentorship has had an effect. Spending time and energy on these connections is an investment, but the relationships you create will provide long-term benefits. Impact work is not a short-term endeavour; to develop knowledge, skills and your own practice in the area is a career-spanning undertaking. Because colleagues are so important in this work (and do not just happen), it is important to be intentional – and sometimes strategic – when creating connections.

INSTITUTIONAL SUPPORTS

In addition to the supports you can get from colleagues, many institutions have resources available for impact work. Some of the institutional supports may be about compliance – for example, ensuring that research impact statements for funders are examined and meet institutional standards – but many are there to support academics to carry out engagement and impact activities. Some are even available to help connect researchers and communities where the impact will be made. However, these resources may not be readily apparent. It may take some work to find the information you need about what is available and how you can access their support.

Again, the field of information science can help you think about the various ways you can access the information you need. There are four main ways that people find information: active seeking (actively look for information, such as searching a university website), active scanning (identifying a likely information source or person and pay attention, such as signing up for a regular newsletter), non-directed monitoring (serendipitously encountering useful information, such as someone overhearing a conversation discussing useful information) and by proxy (being identified as someone who needs information and having someone else provide that information to you) (McKenzie, 2003). Colleagues can help providing you with information by proxy (particularly if they know you are interested in impact work) but you can do a lot by starting to look for information yourself.

What You Need

One thing that can help as you start your impact work is to try to get the lay of the land. Understanding the impact landscape can help you plan and be strategic with your own work and position yourself to take advantage of what resources are available.

It is useful to look at government priorities to determine if there is alignment between your own values and where the government is investing resources. Often, public funding agencies have priority areas that are aligned with the government's, in addition to specific requirements regarding impact work in grants. For example, Canada's Social Sciences and Humanities Research Council (SSHRC) has 16 Global Challenges (SSHRC, 2022) that range from *Inhabiting Challenging Environments* to *The Arts Transformed*. These areas are often quite broad, and positioning your own work within one of the areas can help demonstrate the importance of your work to what the government and funders want to accomplish. Most universities also have priorities, which may be written as research priorities, themes, focus areas or strategies. Being able to speak about your work in the context of government, funder, and university priorities and strategies – and to specifically demonstrate how it addresses these priorities – may help you to access institutional supports. Some universities have dedicated research impact units or supports related to impact in various offices throughout the institution. It is useful to identify the places where support is available.

Once you have identified where the supports exist, it is useful to take note of the types of support, which are typically personnel, training and specialised funding. Where there are people whose job is to work with scholars one-on-one to help them plan out their research impact, utilise them. Many universities also provide training to groups, often in relation to requirements in a funding application. Many universities will also have internal funding calls to help support establish research impact projects. If you're early in your academic career, it is not too early so start getting familiar with the research impact landscape.

How to Do It

Actively seeking information using your university website is a very good place to start. It is useful to make note of what your university calls impact work – research impact, innovation, knowledge exchange, knowledge mobilisation, community engagement, etc. – to help guide your search.

From there, you want to identify which offices or units have to do with engagement and impact work, including industry engagement, knowledge exchange, or knowledge mobilisation units. Some faculties may also have their own impact staff. Common offices and units across the university include the research office, media and communications office, and the library. Explore which units have dedicated impact staff and see what supports they offer. Many offices will have newsletters and alerts that you can subscribe to. Others may have events and workshops to attend. Where dedicated support is not available, you may find skills relating to engagement pathways and impact generation in professional staff in other areas such as marketing, alumni relations, events, etc. If there are less formalised offerings, emailing specific staff members who you identify and asking to meet with them can be a great way to get to know them and what they can offer.

From personal experience in putting together a grant application that requires a robust research impact plan, I would recommend having a quick meeting with impact staff early to get ideas from them. They will have worked with lots of scholars and seen lots of examples of impactful projects. Starting your conversations early will help you to better integrate your impact work into the plan – and allocate appropriate budget to it.

While some services and supports will be free (such as identifying sources of funding), other supports will require money (such as turning research findings into a short digital animation to share on social media). The impact environment at your institution may be quite scattered, so attending events and speaking with colleagues (as discussed above) will also be an important way to identify what resources and supports are available.

PROFESSIONAL DEVELOPMENT

It can be tempting to think that because we are skilled in research that we are also automatically skilled in research impact work. However, for most academics, research impact was not a part of their master's or doctoral studies. So, while we are skilled in research, carrying out research impact projects requires time and effort to develop knowledge, skills and networks that go in to make successful projects.

For many academics, impact work also requires a shift in orientation and ways of thinking about our work. Impact projects can be viewed as a project inside a project that requires another set of skills and methods, separate from the research itself. We all need to ask ourselves what skills are needed to carry out research impact projects and whether or not we have those skills. Then we need to determine what skills we can develop (e.g. acquiring new writing skills to write for a general audience) and what we should leave to other professionals (e.g. digital animation). Once we've assessed our skills, there are numerous places to undertake professional development.

As discussed, institutions often provide information and training sessions on impact. Disciplinary and professional associations frequently provide workshops. Increasingly, there are conferences and other events devoted to impact. Not only are there many useful places to gain new skills, but they are great places to build and foster your research impact networks.

Research engagement and impact work are of vital importance and can be incredibly rewarding for ourselves, as well as the communities we engage with. Identifying and leveraging collegial and institutional supports can help us accomplish our work. It is just important to keep in mind that acquiring new skills and shifting our orientation to incorporate impact work into our research projects won't happen overnight. Each activity you undertake, new connection made and understanding you obtain adds to and shapes your own impact practices. This is how an impactful academic can navigate complex organisations to increase the impact of their work, not only within the context of a project, but in the span of a career. Each new connection you make and skill you acquire over your career is a new colour added to your palette that can help you paint the picture of the impact your research can have.

Fostering Impact

For those who are in positions of authority – heads of academic units, supervisors of doctoral students, senior scholars – it is helpful to recognise the ways in which you can help to foster impact work within your sphere of influence. A major part of this is to think of ways to decrease barriers.

One way to decrease barriers is to be a source of information for those who are part of your professional network. Staying up-to-date on what is happening with research impact within your institution and disciplinary association will allow you at act as a proxy – to pass along the information to those you know who are interested.

It is incredibly helpful to create a list of key information resources and supports where more junior colleagues and students can go for information. A list that is a 'one stop shop' and curated by you to include only the most important can be incredibly helpful in taking the guess work out of where someone should start their quest for research impact information and resources.

Another way to decrease barriers is to act as a mentor – particularly collaborating with junior colleagues and students and allowing them opportunities to actively engage in impact work. Scaffolding them through the process of carrying out a research impact project can help them to shift their orientation towards impact work being an integral, habitual part of their research projects.

REFERENCES

Cross, R., & Sproull, L. (2004). More than an answer: Information relationships for actionable knowledge. *Organization Science*, *15*(4), 446–462. https://doi.org/10.1287/orsc.1040.0075

Fisher, K. E. (2005). Information grounds. In K. E. Fisher, S. Erdelez, & L. E. F. McKechnie (Eds.), *Theories of information behavior* (pp. 185–190). Published for the American Society for Information Science and Technology by Information Today.

McKenzie, P. J. (2003). A model of information practices in accounts of everyday-life information seeking. *Journal of Documentation, 59*(1), 19–40. https://doi.org/10.1108/00220410310457993

Miller, F. Q. (2015). Experiencing information use for early career academics' learning: A knowledge ecosystem model. *Journal of Documentation, 71*(6), 1228–1249. https://doi.org/10.1108/JD-04-2014-0058

Social Science and Humanities Research Council. (2022). Imagining Canada's future: 16 Global challenges. https://www.sshrc-crsh.gc.ca/funding-financement/programs-programmes/challenge_areas-domaines_des_defis/index-eng.aspx

Willson, R. (2016). *Information in transition: Examining the information behaviour of academics as they transition into university careers.* Doctoral thesis, Charles Sturt University. https://researchoutput.csu.edu.au/ws/portalfiles/portal/9316538

Willson, R. (2018). "Systemic Managerial Constraints": How universities influence the information behaviour of HSS early career academics. *Journal of Documentation, 74*(4), 862–879. https://doi.org/10.1108/JD-07-2017-0111

3

STRATEGIC DIGITAL ENGAGEMENT FOR IMPACT: BUILDING YOUR ACADEMIC PRESENCE ONLINE

Erika E. Smith and Richard Hayman

ABSTRACT

In today's digital environments, online engagement is a critical component of achieving successful, sustainable impact. Building an online presence that extends beyond the walls of academia is therefore an essential part of developing as a scholar during any stage of the career span. In this chapter, we discuss career-wide approaches for establishing yourself as a "networked scholar" (Goodier & Czerniewicz, 2015) to build connections and foster communication. We also explore ways to engage your audience through open, public outputs (publications, graphics, websites, profile tools, etc.). Using the key strategies presented, scholars can build an online academic presence and increase their scholarly visibility on the web or through social media. At the core of this chapter is an exploration of how academics can develop and communicate about themselves and their research interests, to achieve their goals both in the near-term and across their career span. While the approaches presented are not prescriptive, they are intended to encourage the reader to generate a plan for online engagement that helps establish their scholarly identity. These tried and tested activities can be leveraged for engaging different audiences in research in ways that promote networked scholarship and create pathways to impact.

Keywords: Networked scholarship; digital engagement; social media; academic development; scholarly communication; knowledge mobilization; academic communities

INTRODUCTION

In our work with academics, we often hear that people are either too busy, or just plain uncomfortable, to engage with the idea of being an impactful academic and promoting meaningful use of their work as a networked scholar. But researchers put a lot of time and energy into scholarship, from project design to data analysis, to reporting, and publishing findings. Shouldn't some of that time and energy also be spent sharing this work in ways that interested audiences can find and make use of it? We want our scholarship to be impactful, and we want people to engage with the new knowledge created, so it is surely worth the effort to ensure that others can easily find and connect with us and our work.

Of course, making an impact doesn't simply mean publishing or otherwise sharing our work. We can see impact in action when people understand, experience, or do things differently based on their interactions with academics and their outputs (University of York, n.d.).

Today, the ever-evolving academic job market and the research funding landscape means there are increased expectations to show impacts tangibly. Greater emphasis is now placed not only on demonstrating the quality and scholarly significance of your research but also on mobilizing and translating your work for a variety of audiences, and across a diversity of contexts, including online environments.

Effective use of digital engagement strategies can help researchers to promote prospective and actual use of their work and capture impactful examples of how their contributions foster positive change for individuals, partners, and communities. By interactively sharing your work more widely across audiences within and beyond academia, you can develop your expertise and reputation while at the same time fostering impact in a broader context.

Engaging Online: Creating Pathways to Impact

Digital engagement has become essential for cultivating, understanding, and defining the impact of your work. Online environments are now a necessary part of extending your expertise through different networks, increasing the findability of publications and other outputs, and connecting with relevant users and audiences – all of which are necessary pathways to impact.

Whether you're an early career researcher or a senior scholar, establishing your presence and engaging online is now part of being an academic. When done intentionally and strategically, time spent on these efforts can be a useful investment in yourself and your career. Developing your online presence and meaningfully engaging as a networked scholar can foster worthwhile and rewarding interactions that create the conditions for impact to occur across your career span.

BEING (OR BECOMING) A NETWORKED SCHOLAR

What does it mean to be a networked scholar? Social media researcher Veletsianos (2016) describes these scholars as those "who make use of participatory technologies and online social networks to share, improve, validate, and further their scholarship" (p. 2). Many forms of research and scholarship today require this engagement with online networks, especially for those concerned with broadening their impact.

At the heart of this idea of networked scholarship is the importance of building new online connections and relationships. For many scholars, those online networks are (or will soon become) a critical part of their academic profile and are inherently involved in mobilizing and translating their work.

Building Blocks of a Networked Scholar

So how can you develop as (or become) a networked scholar? Consider your own work in the context of the seven interconnected facets shown in the building blocks below (Fig. 1 by Goodier & Czerniewicz, 2015):

Fig. 1. Building Blocks of the Networked Scholar. *Note:* **Seven interconnected facets of being a networked scholar. The original image appears on page 6 of Goodier, S. & Czerniewicz, L. (2015).** *Academics' online presence: A four-step guide to taking control of your visibility* **(3rd ed.). University of Cape Town. http://open.uct.ac.za/handle/ 11427/2652**

The building blocks provide a useful framework for developing and extending your academic work through web and social networks. While there isn't a prescriptive way to achieve all these elements, below we describe key approaches to identity, presence, and reputation through pathways to visibility and by developing your academic profile. We also outline approaches involving groups, conversations, connections, and sharing in our sections on digital engagement and using social media.

For each of the building blocks, ask yourself: where are your strengths and where are the opportunities for growth?

You may find that you're a novice in one block but have existing strengths in another. Leverage these strengths while working on those areas that need improvement.

MAKING YOURSELF VISIBLE

Engagement begins by forging connections yourself and being open and available to connections and invitations from others. Your online academic presence is the primary way that other academics will discover your teaching, research, and scholarly interests and expertise. While publications might be a main source for this, when it comes specifically to engagement, the information others can find about you on web pages, social media sites, digital publication venues, and other platforms is fundamental. It's important to know what this looks like currently and where you'd like it to grow.

Evaluate Your Current Online Presence

Before starting to actively develop your academic presence, the first step is to determine how visible you are online currently by doing a simple online search. Yes, this means you need to search for yourself online and take a good look at what you find.

> **Exercise: Search yourself**
> Google yourself: Enter your name in a search engine to find out how you appear online. Then ask:
>
> - Do the top search results show you and your academic (or professional) work?
>
>   –If not, why not? What do you like, and what would you like to change?

–Discuss the search results with a trusted friend or colleague (ideally one from outside your discipline). What input or suggestions do they have?

- Can people from within and outside of academia, including media outlets and potential partners, easily find clear information about your areas of expertise and contributions?

  –Is your contact information up to date and easily viewable?

  –Is there a way to connect with you on a social media platform?

  –Can people see examples of your research, teaching, or speaking?

- Where do you see any opportunities to improve or enhance the results?

- Does searching for yourself online showcase you, your interests, and your research in the ways that you want them to appear?

This simple search exercise should give you a good idea of why it might be valuable to focus on building your online presence. Use this exercise to make a plan that prioritizes areas where you want to increase visibility and engage in relevant scholarly networks (Goodier & Czerniewicz, 2015; La Trobe University Research Education and Development Team, n.d.).

DEVELOPING YOUR ACADEMIC PROFILES

Now that you have an idea of how you already appear online, it's time to consider how you want to expand this presence and define your identity. We always recommend developing a couple of online academic profiles that can serve as a foundation for engaging in a broader range of other networked scholarly activities. You can then develop and connect these profile tools, like ORCID or Google Scholar, to other online engagement spaces, such as your web and social media presence.

Visibility and Findability, With a Focus on You

First and foremost, your online presence should reflect you and your work in the ways that you want them to be known. Ultimately, this approach recognizes that you are the best person to define how you and your research appear online. Goodier and Czerniewicz (2015) remind us that you may not be in full control of your *digital shadow*, or the "content about you posted and uploaded by others, or even created by you inadvertently" (p. 5), but the exercise above asking you to search for yourself online should provide some critical awareness of your existing digital footprint. This will hopefully lead you to some informed decisions about how you can shape that presence going forward.

This focus-on-you approach also means you get to decide what accomplishments to highlight. For instance, you might want to focus on profiling yourself as comprehensively and completely as possible, likely by showcasing your career progression and contributions over time. Or, you might decide to take a more selective approach, perhaps by highlighting specific periods of your career or by focusing on key projects or publications.

When it comes to your approach, do what's comfortable, keeping your career stage in mind. Arguably, early career academics have an advantage here, since at this point you may not have a lifetime of contributions to highlight, or much of a digital shadow to reshape. Your initial online presence might start small, but with regular care and maintenance, it will grow throughout your whole career.

RECOMMENDED STRATEGIES FOR ONLINE VISIBILITY

Whenever we work with researchers interested in enhancing their online presence, we recommend establishing two key academic profiles before anything else: your Google Scholar profile (GSP), and your ORCID identity record. While there are many online scholarly profile tools to choose from, we recommend networked scholars explore these options first. These two tools will form the backbone of your online presence and how easily others will find you. The following is not a how-to guide for setup – instructions are readily found online – but rather a brief overview of key features and reasons why we recommend these tools first.

Google Scholar Profiles

Creating your GSP is our go-to recommendation for those looking to establish their online presence. If nothing else, it's free and costs nothing but a bit of time, while being the easiest and fastest way to enhance your online visibility. Having a Google Scholar profile makes it much easier for others to find you and your research due to the indexing and search features of Google. You can keep your profile private while you complete the initial setup to your tastes, and make it public once you're ready to share. Those who view your public GSP profile will see your research interests, affiliations, and links to your publications. Plus, future updates to your profile can be automated entirely, or you can activate notifications to receive a message when Google Scholar finds possible works to add to your profile.

Since it's drawing on works indexed by Google Scholar, the coverage is comprehensive and will find your publications appearing in journals, as monographs, book chapters, theses or dissertations, conference proceedings, and occasional grey literature (such as your contributions to reports, to government or policy documents, or to other expert, non-academic publications). It can also be used for identifying your presentations and workshops. You can automate this search, or manually add research outputs. Because it's Google, these sources will link out to an online version of your work and generally provide better coverage than you would find in one of the more traditional (paid) citation tools (e.g., Scopus or Web of Science).

> **Tip: Automation is Useful, but Requires Checks**
> If you decide to fully automate the process of adding artifacts to any of your scholarly profiles, plan to periodically review and clean up the additions. The automation tools aren't perfect and may add artifacts that aren't actually your contributions. You'll want to ensure that these false hits weren't added incorrectly and that nothing is missing from your profile.

Your GSP shows traditional impact measures of your works through citations, including total (known) citations to all artifacts captured in your profile, the h-index for those publications, and also the i10-index. All of these are important measures since they are citation counts at the *author level*, meaning they directly reflect that your work has been cited and thus impacted other research in some way. In addition, GSP focuses on the last five years, so that you can see your recent impact. These measures are easily verifiable, since the citation counts link to the known citing articles for each artifact. This is a window on your impact through traditional research metrics. We talk about other metrics later.

Finally, as a networked scholar, you will want to take advantage of features of your profile that create connections to other researchers. There's an option to verify your email address officially connected to an academic institution or research organization, options to link to your personal website or other preferred site, and the ability to tag your coauthors and collaborators, immediately connecting to their Scholar profiles (if they have one). Finally, if you use keywords to define your areas of interest, these will become hyperlinked searches that will connect you with other researchers interested in the same topics.

Open Researcher and Contributor ID

Claiming your ORCID profile is also free and easy to setup. Importantly, ORCID helps address possible confusion around identifying authorship through name disambiguation. Consider: is your name truly unique? Academia is no exception to the problem of common and shared names, and so it's worth ensuring that your contributions are always connected to you.

HELLO
My Name Is

https://orcid.org/
0000-0002-4957-705X

ORCID helps address this problem through *authority control*, simply by organizing contributions made by a single entity (you, the creator) and assigning and collecting them under a specific and unique identifier (a persistent URL). This persistent identifier leads to an online profile that you control and maintain, ensuring you remain the authoritative voice on your research profile.

ORCID is particularly useful if some of your contributions appeared under a different name than your current or preferred moniker, such as after a name change due to marital status, gender expression, a cultural or religious preference, or a myriad of other reasons. ORCID also helps in cases where even the correct display of your name isn't fully under your control, such as when publications use name variants (e.g., full names versus initials) and you want to be sure these permutations all still identify you.

Additional benefits of ORCID include enriched profile options where you can authoritatively highlight other contributions around your research career. Rather than just focusing on publications, you can include your grants, significant awards, and distinctions, and indicate your education and employment history. Plus, the ORCID privacy settings are quite granular, such that you can control how much information in each category is visible. As a networked scholar you will also want to explore the options for linking to your other online profiles; to make sure people can easily find and distinguish your social media accounts; and to easily find your website and connect to your other academic profiles.

Finally, your ORCID can save you time, thanks to the ORCID organization's commitment to interoperability and standardization. Many journal publishers, funding bodies, university systems, and other research dissemination and support tools now require you to provide your ORCID as part of the submission or application process. These platforms will connect to and read basic information from your ORCID profile, meaning you don't have to spend the effort to populate forms and metadata repeatedly – maintain it all in your ORCID profile and let it do the work of completing those forms for you.

Top 5 Academic Profile Options

When considering what profiles to develop, here are our recommendations for where to start:

- Google Scholar = https://scholar.google.ca/citations

- ORCID = https://orcid.org/

- ResearchGate = https://www.researchgate.net/

- LinkedIn = https://www.linkedin.com/

- Publons/ResearcherID = https://publons.com/about/home

You don't have to develop a profile in every space. In fact, profile fatigue is real (Allen, 2017), and we recommend *against* trying to be present in all of them.

Sharing: Let's Talk About Access

After you have established your online profile and made progress toward building your online connections, it's time to give some consideration to sharing, especially the ways that others will access your published research and other information about the projects you want to promote. More specifically, we recommend making your artifacts as open and publicly accessible as possible.

Can your intended audience access the full publication you promoted with a Tweet, or added to your Google Scholar profile? Remember that subscriptions, paywalls, and many other factors can affect the accessibility of valuable research findings. These can pose major barriers for a variety of information users inside and beyond academia, and are particularly challenging for communities, organizations, and members of the public.

In other words, ensuring that those who need, want, or might otherwise benefit from the research can access it is part of being a networked scholar, and making your work widely accessible for the long term is part of catalyzing impact. Not only will your research be available to more people, but considerable research shows that open publications (e.g., open access, open data, and open education resources) are read and cited more often than their subscription-locked counterparts. So, it's also in your best interest to make sure your outputs are freely and openly available whenever it's feasible to do so.

CREATING A ROADMAP FOR DIGITAL ENGAGEMENT

Most of the time, engagement doesn't just happen – it requires some intentional effort and planning. Drafting a brief roadmap where you identify strategies for using web and social media platforms, and allocating time for achieving your goals, will help to focus your efforts on engagement that's of the greatest value. We recommend that your roadmap for digital engagement consider the following.

Focus on What's Most Valuable

Who are the individuals and groups that can use, benefit from, and inform your work? How do *you* want *your research* and expertise to be adopted? What is the value of your work for audiences within and outside of academia? How you find value in focusing your time and efforts online should directly relate to how you want to define yourself as an impactful academic. The more specific you can be in visioning what engagement and impact look like for you, the better. Focusing on what's most valuable – from your perspective and in the eyes of your audience – will help you not only to extend your own profile but also to find and engage with interested colleagues, stakeholders, and partners online in strategic ways.

Set Achievable Goals

What do you want to achieve with your online presence? For instance, do you want to increase the visibility of your profile as a researcher? Or to have your work in a particular area reach new audiences? Start by creating one or two goals that are specific, measurable, achievable, realistic, and time-based (SMART) to guide your digital engagement plan. Revisit these goals to check your progress on a regular basis.

Identify Key Audiences and Spaces

The vast number of online spaces make it impossible to effectively engage in all of them, so aim for quality over quantity. Begin dedicating your efforts in one or two key digital spaces by identifying who your main audience is and understanding what online platforms they use. For example, you might create an infographic that mobilizes and translates key research findings, then invite key stakeholders or potential future partners to discuss it on Twitter or LinkedIn.

Remember that long-form content created for a blog, e-newsletter, or website should be formatted and presented differently on social platforms that focus on brevity and audiovisuals, such as Instagram, Twitter, or TikTok. Be sure to align your engagement goals with content strategies that ensure your use of text and media are effective for your audience and the specific online environment.

Allocate Time for Updates and Communication

Being findable online means ensuring your profile on university and professional websites, and on social media sites, is current. Schedule regular "tune-up" times to refresh your online academic profiles, even by setting a recurring calendar reminder.

Distributing too much one-way content can turn people off. Remember that meaningful online engagement requires responsive, two-way interaction about not only your own work but also the work of others. Your audience will usually be looking for timely, authentic back-and-forth communication, so plan time for engaging in discussions and posting comments or responses when using social platforms.

Being selective and strategic by focusing your efforts on your top goals will help to make your online engagement more effective and manageable.

Did you Know?
Many post-secondary institutions have media experts who can consult on communication strategies and recommend effective approaches, including web and social media strategies. Consider reaching out to your university's communications team to gain feedback on your digital engagement plan.

USING SOCIAL MEDIA

As with social media generally, academic use of social media comes with many pros and cons. For example, some scholars are surprised when their work goes viral, while others work in areas that can be a lightning rod for trolls and controversy (see Carrigan, 2019). Choosing whether and how to use social media as a networked scholar is ultimately up to you. However, just as with the online platforms above, it is our belief that there is value in being an active part of the conversation on social media, rather than passively allowing others to shape these conversations for you.

Social media is a useful way to extend your reach in academic networks. Beyond the individual reputational benefit, as Carrigan and Fatsis aptly note in a recent interview (University of Cambridge, 2021), it is important to foster rich engagement by using social media for the public good, instead of using it to simply broadcast information passively to a public audience. With this very kind of rich engagement in mind, the following three steps provide recommendations for ways to start interacting through groups, conversations, connections, and sharing on social media.

Three Steps for Social Media Engagement

Choose

Choose *one or two* social media platforms that can best reach your audience, where you can see yourself being active and engaged. Examples of popular social platforms for networked academics include Twitter, LinkedIn, ResearchGate, Facebook, and Instagram.

When creating your accounts, be sure to complete all the relevant fields, especially your bio line and profile picture.

Decide if you want to focus on your academic persona distinct from any personal accounts you might have (usually a good idea). Ask a trusted friend to review things and give you constructive feedback before you go live.

Observing different social media habits of colleagues and partners on your chosen platform can be useful. What works well and gains traction? Such examples will help you determine which social media practices you might want to emulate, and those to avoid.

Connect

Connect by "following" or "friending" individuals or organizations with similar interests and areas of expertise on each platform you join. This will help you find and curate content that relates to your academic identity. Make note of relevant accounts, groups, pages, or lists that you could follow, comment on, post about, or redistribute – especially ones that share easily consumed media-rich links, images, and videos that engage people with added auditory or visual elements.

Learn the format or "anatomy" of posts on your social media spaces to increase findability and engagement through mentions (often using the @ symbol) and hashtags (typically using #).

Interact

Share and promote timely information with your network on a regular basis, ideally in ways that invite discussion. It's okay to shine a light on your own valuable work, as well as the excellent work of others.

An account that has been abandoned is a liability because it can give the wrong impression that your work has been discontinued, or increase your risk of missing messages, mentions, and other notifications. Commit to being active on a regular basis (weekly, daily, etc.). Knowing what you want to share and when will help you plan. It's better to not be on a social media service than to present yourself poorly or partly.

Being consistent in your messaging in ways that reinforce your expertise and interests will let your audience know what to expect by following you and what you bring. As you establish your voice and reputation, your messages and interactions should be consistent with your desired online academic profile more often than not, at least initially.

The type and quality of interactions matter. Have an engagement strategy that fosters interaction through chats, discussions, questions, or polls and adds interest by using links, attachments, or visuals. If you know an output (article, report, etc.) will be published soon, plan ahead for ways to promote and build engagement with it on social media.

Timing is a critical part of social media engagement. Set aside refresh time, such as regularly scheduling social media "tune-up Tuesdays." Some systems (e.g., HootSuite) can post content on preset dates and times, but use these with caution: the immediate, up-to-the-minute nature of social media still requires you to make time for prompt interactions and responses.

There isn't one recipe for success with social media. The choices you make in becoming a networked scholar are ultimately up to you. Be strategic about where you focus your engagement efforts and do what works for you in authentically achieving your goals.

CAPTURING ENGAGEMENT AND IMPACT

To know if you're on the right track to achieving your goals, it's important to keep track of how your digital engagement is developing to both see your progress over time and have meaningful examples at your fingertips.

Capturing engagement and impact can be as simple as keeping a living document listing a running tally of examples of your contributions being discussed or used via links or screenshots. If these are difficult to find, consider asking for testimonials, recommendations, or impact stories from the communities you've connected with in your scholarly networks. As you're applying for jobs, funding, or awards, you'll be surprised how helpful it is to refer to illustrative use cases that present a clear picture of how you interact and promote change with different audiences.

ENGAGEMENT METRICS

You can track digital engagement over time through *alternative metrics*, commonly known as altmetrics. To be clear, altmetrics are not citations. Instead, they are quantitative and qualitative measures of how others have engaged with and used your research outputs and ideas outside of traditional academic venues. Altmetrics track online engagement, including social media attention (e.g., sharing and mentions of your work on Twitter or Facebook), online views and downloads of your publications, or when your work has been added to or bookmarked in certain reference managers (e.g., Mendeley). And like traditional metrics, altmetrics are cumulative and show development over time.

Capturing these metrics on social and web engagement makes it clear when someone has found, shared, or discussed your work. Considering that use of your research by community groups, policy-makers, and government reports typically are not shown in traditional impact measures, altmetrics can be particularly important for capturing engagement beyond academic contexts. If someone is Tweeting about your work, that's engagement! Use this as a starting place to join the conversation.

Some Options for Altmetrics
Several platforms can be used for altmetrics. Here are some free and paid options.

- Impact Story (free) = https://profiles.impactstory.org/

- Kudos (free) = https://info.growkudos.com/

- Altmetric (paid/subscription) = https://www.altmetric.com/

- Plum Analytics (paid/subscription) = http://www.plumanalytics.com/

- Overton (paid/subscription) = https://www.overton.io/

Individually and together, traditional and alternative metrics can help you to get a sense of the trends and interest around a particular research output or set of ideas, so it's worthwhile to be aware of these throughout your career. Also, important to keep in mind is that all metrics have limitations and may only tell part of your engagement story. Any information detailing how people are engaging with and using your work is more important than how many might have simply seen it.

CONCLUSION

Being online is now an essential part of any academic career, especially for those interested in generating impact through their work across their career span. But while we may be required to be online, the amount of energy and effort spent on these activities – and the types of digital engagement that take priority – are up to us.

Creating pathways to impact is about more than the number of downloads, followers, likes, or shares. It's about using our capabilities as networked scholars for connecting people within and beyond academia to build new understandings, experiences, and approaches in ways that lead to positive changes in the world around us.

REFERENCES

Allen, E. (2017, September 29). Researcher #profilefatigue – what it is and why it's exhausting! [blog post]. *ScienceOpen*. https://blog.scienceopen.com/2014/09/researcher-profilefatigue-what-it-is-and-why-its-exhausting/

Carrigan, M. (2019). *Social media for academics* (2nd ed.). Sage.

Goodier, S., & Czerniewicz, L. (2015). *Academics' online presence: A four-step guide to taking control of your visibility* (3rd ed.). University of Cape Town. http://open.uct.ac.za/handle/11427/2652

La Trobe University Research Education and Development Team. (n.d.). The digital academic module. https://v3.pebblepad.com.au/spa/#/public/yqqhw74MqfrHgpHW3bRnrx48gh

University of Cambridge. (2021, July 8). Why academics need to organise, collectivise, and 'socialise' social media. *Faculty of Education News*. https://www.educ.cam.ac.uk/facultyweb_content/news/go-platform-why-academicsneed-to-organise

University of York. (n.d.). What is research impact? https://www.york.ac.uk/staff/research/research-impact/impactdefinition/

Veletsianos, G. (2016). *Social media in academia: Networked scholars*. Routledge.

4

WRITING IMPACT FOR GRANTS: PACK YOUR BAGS. WE ARE GOING ON AN IMPACT JOURNEY!

Lucy Jowett and Alisha Peart

ABSTRACT

In this chapter, we share our top tips on writing impact for funding bids and reports. These are drawn from our extensive experience working across a UK university as research impact managers and also successfully developing and writing small to multimillion-pound grant applications for UK charity, UK Government and European funding. We have developed and delivered impact training to researchers at all career stages, written impact case studies for the UK's research assessment and published on the genre.[1] We also lead the Impact Special Interest Group for the UK's Association of Research Managers and Administrators (ARMA) and contribute to conferences and specialist training internationally, which has included the Australasia region, Africa and Europe.

Keywords: Impact; writing; funding; grants; proposal;
reports; research; application; statement; pathway;
planning; beneficiary; stakeholder; monitoring; evaluation; higher education

In this chapter, we share our top tips on writing impact for
funding bids and reports. These are drawn from our extensive
experience working across a UK university as research impact
managers and also successfully developing and writing small to
multimillion-pound grant applications for UK charity, UK
Government and European funding. We have developed and
delivered impact training to researchers at all career stages,
written impact case studies for the UK's research assessment
and published on the genre.[2] We also lead the Impact Special
Interest Group for the UK's Association of Research Managers
and Administrators (ARMA) and contribute to conferences and
specialist training internationally, which has included the
Australasia region, Africa and Europe.

The difference your research could make to the world
beyond academia is a journey you, and your research will go
on over the lifetime of your career. Securing funding for your
research and the activities that will make it impactful underpins this. Here we look at approaches that will help you to
maximise the impact elements of your funding proposals.

Writing effectively about impact is an emerging genre, and
it is increasingly critical to the success of your research grant
applications or retrospective research project reports.[3] The
temptation can be to leave impact to the end of the writing
process and treat it as an add-on to your carefully crafted
funding applications. But this will not do your applications

justice. Funders are increasingly focussing on impact, and they want to understand the difference your research may make. They often require prospective impact statements making your plans for proposed pathways to impact explicit as a stand-alone element of your proposal. In some cases, for example, UK research councils, impact is integrated into the body of the application by weaving it throughout the document. Other funders require project reports which describe impact retro-spectively; they want to know what has changed due to your research and how you have engaged with stakeholders. Being able to describe and evidence impact is important, so what is the best approach to take and what techniques are there for writing and testing impact statements that will help you to succeed? We suggest framing your approach by using the analogy of planning a trip that forms part of your research career's journey – so pack your bags; we're on our way!

EVERY JOURNEY IS UNIQUE

Sometimes researchers assume there is 'boiler plate text' for impact. There isn't. In the UK's 2014 research assessment (Research Excellence Framework), there were over 3,700 unique pathways to impact![4] Every research project you undertake will have its own distinctive pathways to impact, and there is no 'one size fits all' when it comes to writing about impact. Your impact statement should never be cut and paste from a previous application. The approach you take needs to be tailored to the specific project and the point where you are in the journey. Research funders and their reviewers want to know that, as a researcher, you understand the mechanisms that can generate impact. With thousands of potential pathways to impact, which routes will you explore?

A CAREER JOURNEY WITH IMPACT – WHAT IS YOUR STARTING POINT, AND WHERE WILL YOU GO?

Take a step back and look at how your next funding application will contribute to your career-long impact journey. What are the activities in your proposal that will move you along that route? This funding may enable you to engage with key stakeholders for the first time. It may extend your reach by applying previous research to a new problem with new target beneficiaries. Whilst your next proposal will focus on this part of your career journey as a researcher, don't forget to talk about where you have come from. Demonstrating your previous experience shows you know what you are doing and that you have a track record of delivery.

TOP TIP: BEFORE YOU GO, RESEARCH THE BEST ROUTE – KNOW YOUR FUNDER

The key is to understand, precisely, your funder's motivations in relation to impact. This will help you to craft the way you describe impact in your funding bid to maximise your chances of success.

Impact may be important to your funders for one or more of the following: accountability in spending public money and demonstrating the benefits of that investment to society; improving research quality through engaging with potential beneficiaries; maximising benefits by shortening the time to realising benefits; and/or increasing the impact funders' investments have made.

The way you plan your route depends on what type of funding you are applying for. This will vary depending on your career stage and the size of grant you are seeking. You may be looking at seed funding from local sources, for example, your faculty or school. This is likely to be short-term and aimed at small, achievable impacts or to facilitate critical first-time engagements with stakeholders or beneficiaries. Having two-way engagement with the right people will help you determine the right direction for your research, forming the basis for larger funding applications. Seed funding can lead to other funding, and this is part of the impact journey.

You may seek funding from research councils, businesses, charities, or government sources that are likely to have different timescales, geographic scales (local, national or international), differing amounts of funding available, and differing expectations of the number and type of partners that you will involve. Funders expect to see impact plans commensurate with these elements, so be transparent in your approach. Your plan needs to be realistic, convincing and honest with the reviewer, particularly in considering how much time and effort your impact activities and evidence gathering will take. Describe your existing experience in engaging with your target beneficiaries or stakeholders and avoid over-claiming or over-blowing your expertise.

TOP TIP: TIME TO PACK YOUR BAGS AND MAKE SURE YOU HAVE INCLUDED ESSENTIAL ITEMS – DOES YOUR PROPOSAL MATCH WHAT THE FUNDER IS REALLY LOOKING FOR?

Take some time to read the guidance for your funding call and get to know what the reviewers will be looking for. It is important to understand your audience. Ensure that you focus your impact text on what is specified by the funding call. Sometimes impact is prominent in assessment criteria. In others, the focus is on engagement or knowledge exchange. Funders may be looking for international or policy impacts, impact on health or the economy; some funders may require measurable impact goals – so you need to be able to monitor and evaluate them. Whatever the funder is looking for is what you must provide.

A useful way of framing your impact plans appropriate to the scale of funding, and your funder's interests, is to use the concepts of 'significance' and 'reach'. These were coined by the UK's Research Excellence Framework (REF). Reach is the extent and diversity of beneficiaries that have been affected by the research, while significance is the degree of change for those beneficiaries.

Once you have written impact into your funding application, play a round of 'buzz word bingo' – this involves checking that you are reflecting the language and terms used by the funder in their guidance. At the same time, and this can be tricky, use plain language and keep it simple. Ensure that you do not use impenetrable acronyms or technical terms without explanation; it is possible that your proposal will be read by lay panel members or by non-experts in your field. Do not assume detailed prior knowledge of the subject area. To test this, try explaining your impact statement to someone else, perhaps a non-expert in your field, and ask them to paraphrase it back. This can help you identify gaps in logic and issues with clarity.[5]

Funders have been known to send different sections of a proposal to different reviewers, so it is important to ensure each section of the application can stand alone and makes sense if read in isolation. Make it easy for reviewers by including something you wrote in a previous section that is also pertinent to another by summarising it again before expanding upon it for the later sections. However, remember to use clear, concise and focussed language to make the best use of word count limits.

TOP TIP: CONSULT A TRAVEL AGENT OR LOCAL GUIDE – SEEK ADVICE AND SUPPORT

If you were planning an exciting trip, you might seek the help of a travel agent or a local guide. Writing funding proposals can feel like a lonely job if you don't involve others, and their advice and support can be invaluable. Getting others to read your work can help you benefit from their perspectives, experiences and insights. Someone with specialist knowledge of impact, such as staff in your research office, are well-versed in this genre of writing. They will have read and written many impact statements and reports, and they can provide invaluable guidance (see chapter 2 for more details on tapping into your professional expertise in your network). Academic colleagues who have successful track records with your funder, and those with more contacts or experience of working with your beneficiaries, can also provide excellent support.

Take the opportunity to read good examples of successful proposals; the research office at your university may be able to help provide these.[6] Remember, as discussed in Chapter 2, the earlier you engage with your research office, the better. They offer more than simply process administration or compliance and have a wealth of expertise. However, just like academics, they also have many demands on their time. So, the earlier you engage with them, the more they will be able to help and add value to your application. Consider speaking to more than one colleague in your research office as they may offer different specialisms such as help with costing your activities, helping you engage with your stakeholders, or providing detailed advice on funders and funding calls.

EXCITING OPPORTUNITIES ALONG THE WAY – WHERE WILL YOU END UP?

At the point of submitting your proposal, you can't predict the impact of your research, but you can consider impact from the outset and recognise that research impacts can develop at any stage in the research life cycle and beyond. Impacts can often stem from unexpected or unintended outcomes. What are the best ways of being ready to maximise these opportunities?

WHAT IS YOUR TRAVEL PLAN?

When your funding application contains a credible pathway to impact, funding panel reviewers are inspired with confidence that you will be able to generate the impacts you aspire to. The more you invest in creating a pathway to impact prior to submitting your bid, the easier it then becomes to turn this into a full impact plan for your funded project. So, start thinking about this as early as possible, leave plenty of time to develop your plan and make it clear and as specific as you can (Fig. 1). Articulate a clear connection between the aims of

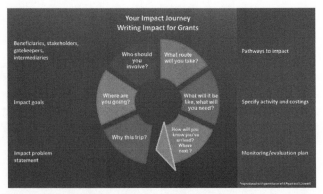

Fig. 1. Your Impact Journey – What to Consider Including When You Write Impact for Grants by A. Peart and L. Jowett.

your research, what the objectives of your impact activities are and what you plan to do.[7]

You can identify the key elements of an impact plan by asking yourself these questions:

- Why do I want to go on this trip? *impact problem statement*;

- What do I want to achieve by going on the trip/where do I want to get to? *impact goals*;

- Who will I need to involve and take with me? *beneficiaries, stakeholders, gatekeepers and intermediaries*;

- What will I do along the way, and how much will it cost? *pathways to impact*; and

- How do I know when I've arrived at my destination? *monitoring/evaluation plan*.

PLANNING YOUR ITINERARY

Impact Problem Statement – Why Do I Want to Go on This Trip?

This should be a clear statement setting out your motivations for the research and its significance. It should include what problems or challenges you want to solve. How do you know there is a problem and a need for change? Who have you engaged with to establish this? What evidence is there of a need for the research?

Impact Goals – What Do I Want to Achieve, and Where Do I Want to Get to?

There may be a variety of goals or milestones along the journey to impact from your proposed research. What are they, what will they look like and when will you realise them? What impacts are appropriate for your research programme across the widest definition of impact, for example, on society, the economy or the environment? Impact can take many years to develop to its full potential, often far beyond funded project timescales. Consider the long term and articulate how you will keep impact going post-project.

DECIDING WHAT TO PACK FOR THE TRIP AND WHO IS COMING WITH YOU

Beneficiaries and Stakeholders – Who Will Be my Travel Companions?

Travel that is immersive, where you really engage with the culture of the place you have gone to, often creates a much more rewarding experience. The same can be said of your impact journey. Questions to ask yourself include: who could potentially benefit from my work, and how will I engage them? Are there intermediaries, and who are they? If I cannot directly engage with the ultimate beneficiaries, who is their advocate or change agent? How will I use existing networks and build new ones?

Collaborative partnerships reassure reviewers that you can deliver; by acknowledging any potential sensitivities, you will also build confidence that your research will be a success. What will you do to ensure that beneficiaries or key stakeholders can engage and stay engaged with your research and help inform it? How can you increase the chances of potential beneficiaries and project partners benefitting from your research? Detailed consideration of stakeholder engagement is contained elsewhere in this book (see chapter 5), but it is worth briefly re-visiting as it is fundamental to writing a successful pathway to impact.

Partnerships, co-design, co-creation and two-way engagement are important mechanisms enabling feedback and helping you to make your approach as useful as possible. These help you facilitate knowledge exchange and create impact from research. If you are considering public engagement as a pathway to impact, remember that two-way engagement is more likely to lead to change than simply outreach or dissemination of your research findings. When you have identified stakeholders that are likely to have a high influence on your research or considerable benefits from it, contact them before finalising your application. Their feedback can create a more credible pathway to impact and enhance their engagement when you come to do the research.

Pathways to Impact – What Activities Will You Do on Your Trip, and How Much Will It Cost?

This is about the practicalities of what you will do to achieve impact. Reviewers want to know *what* activities and costs will help you achieve each one of your impact goals and *how* will you work with beneficiaries? After all, no one will believe you are going on a trip if you haven't prepared the route and know what you need to buy or do to travel along it. An analysis of impact statements in grant applications that resulted in top-rated impacts revealed some useful lessons.[8] These include being as detailed as you can and drawing on your previous experience to demonstrate what you have achieved before. Where possible, include the how, what, who and when in your planning, so, for example, rather than saying you will 'hold meetings', be clear about the type of meetings, with whom and when in the research programme you intend them to take place. Often the key is two-way engagement (rather than simple dissemination of research findings), so describe *how* attendees will provide input. Assign responsibility for specific impact tasks to specific people or groups where possible. Demonstrate flexibility and show you can adapt to the unforeseen; after all, you can't predict the outcomes of your research.

Include project-specific costs relating to the proposed impact activities and impact evaluation in your bid. What resources will you need to put your plan into practice? Cost these and include them in your funding bid where a funder indicates that they are eligible costs. If you don't have experience with costing, engage your research office, who can usually offer costing, contracts and/or consulting expertise.

Monitoring/Evaluation Plan – How Do You Know When You've Arrived?

What will you do to record your starting point and what your destination looks like? How will you demonstrate what changed? How far you travelled (reach) and how important was the trip for the beneficiaries (significance)? Consider how you will measure your success and generate and collect evidence to demonstrate that impact has occurred. Focus on evaluating the change or benefit and also record unintentional change throughout the lifetime of the research project and beyond.

HOW WILL YOU KEEP YOUR TRAVEL COMPANIONS INVOLVED IN YOUR JOURNEY? OR HOW WILL YOU INVOLVE RESEARCH USERS/BENEFICIARIES AT ALL STAGES IN THE RESEARCH LIFECYCLE?

Impact can be demonstrated at every stage of the research lifecycle:

- Short-term: changes in knowledge, attitudes, skills of beneficiaries and uses of research

- Short-term: changes in awareness and engagement of immediate stakeholders

- Medium-term: shifts in practices, policies, strategies, or budget allocations of immediate stakeholders or reaching to wider stakeholder groups

- Long-term: scaling up changes in knowledge, practice, or policies and/or further widening reach

DO YOU KNOW THE WAY? TOP TIP: KNOW YOURSELF – WHAT ARE YOUR SKILLS AND WHAT HELP DO YOU NEED?

So now you know what you want to achieve, what impacts you could create and who you will work with, reflecting on your impact plan, what skills will you need to deliver it? Draw on your transferrable skills and previous experience of impact; build your knowledge; for example, Chapters 5 and 6 address how to work with stakeholders to build and run projects. Identify any skill gaps and address them. Find out what types of support are available to you on campus and beyond to help develop and deliver engagement activities that will generate impact.

NOW YOU'VE ARRIVED!

It takes time and practice to develop your skills in writing effectively in the impact statement genre, but as this develops, you will find that impact becomes ubiquitous, even in proposals where a separate impact statement is not a requirement. We hope that you enjoy a successful, interesting and impactful journey!

NOTES

1. Writing impact case studies: a comparative study of high-scoring and low-scoring case studies from REF2014, (2020), Bella Reichard, Mark S. Reed, Jenn Chubb, Ged Hall, Lucy Jowett, Alisha Peart & Andrea Whittle. https://www.nature.com/articles/s41599-020-0394-7.
2. See footnote 1.
3. See footnote 1.
4. The nature, scale and beneficiaries of research impact, an initial analysis of Research Excellence Framework (REF) 2014 impact case studies, (2015), King's College, London and Digital Science. https://www.kcl.ac.uk/policy-institute/assets/ref-impact.pdf.
5. The Prickly Impact statement, (2021), Dr Wade Kelly. https://researchwhisperer.org/2021/06/01/the-prickly-impact-statement/.

6. 10 lessons from grant proposals that led to the most significand and far-reaching impacts, (2016), Sarah Buckmaster and Prof Mark Reed, https://www.fasttrackimpact.com/post/2016/02/14/pathways-to-topscoring-impacts-an-analysis-of-pathways-to-impact-in-grant-applications.
7. See footnote 6.
8. See footnote 6.

5

TOWARDS IMPACT: BEST PRACTICE IN COMMUNITY AND STAKEHOLDER ENGAGEMENT

Caroline Osborne

ABSTRACT

As academics, quantitative and/or qualitative methods are at the heart of the research we conduct and the insights we seek to share with the world. However, this does not always translate into impactful engagement for the stakeholders and communities we engage with, despite the evidence that indicates the potential to do so. One of the critical ways that academics can generate impact is through community and stakeholder engagement – developing networks and external partnerships that work collaboratively to generate change. Research indicates that more participatory methods of engagement where stakeholders can co-create solutions have the greatest transformational potential for impact. The key to differentiating meaningful and impactful stakeholder engagement from distinct concepts such as communication or consultation is understanding the level of influence the stakeholder will have on the decision. This chapter provides a practical guide for academics to build their practice in impactful engagement throughout their career through eight simple steps. Using the International Association for Public Participation (IAP2) spectrum of public participation, an example of how engagement methods can be selected to build impactful engagement skills throughout the academic career is illustrated. Impactful engagement has the capacity to bring diverse voices and perspectives together to shape decisions and change, and in so doing, create greater impact.

Keywords: Engagement; engaged scholarship; public participation; impact; research methods; community; stakeholder

If you were to delve into the heart of why we choose to pursue the career that we do, many people (academics included) would tell you that they are motivated by the desire to make a difference in the world – to generate meaningful impact.

The world today is complex, and future trends indicate the need for more human-centred design and decision-making (EY, 2020; Taylor et al., 2017). In Australia and internationally, trust in governments and institutions is declining because people simply do not believe they are making decisions in their best interests (Edelman Trust Barometer, 2020, 2021). As outlined by Boyer (1996) in his seminal work *The Scholarship of Engagement*, academics and higher education institutions have a critical role in bringing their intellectual capital and resources to bear on our most pressing issues, through the virtuous cycle of research, teaching and engagement.

One of the critical ways that academics can generate impact is through community and stakeholder engagement – developing networks and external partnerships that work collaboratively to generate change. Through collaborative and reciprocal partnerships, academics can leverage the respective assets and strengths of the university to build shared value through engagement and contribute to meaningful impact in the local and global communities they form part of. For an analysis of the themes that emerge from definitions of best practice engagement and the challenges for academics in realising impactful engagement see Osborne et al. (2021).

The key to differentiating meaningful and impactful stakeholder engagement from distinct concepts such as communication or consultation is understanding the level of influence the stakeholder will have on the decision, as outlined in the International Association for Public Participation (IAP2) spectrum of public participation (see Fig. 1). The IAP2 is a globally recognised peak body that seeks to advance and extend the practice of public participation through professional development,

| INCREASING IMPACT ON THE DECISION | | | | |
INFORM	CONSULT	INVOLVE	COLLABORATE	EMPOWER
PUBLIC PARTICIPATION GOAL — To provide the public with balanced and objective information to assist them in understanding the problem, alternatives, opportunities and/or solutions.	To obtain public feedback on analysis, alternatives and/or decisions.	To work directly with the public throughout the process to ensure that public concerns and aspirations are consistently understood and considered.	To partner with the public in each aspect of the decision including the development of alternatives and the identification of the preferred solution.	To place final decision making in the hands of the public.
PROMISE TO THE PUBLIC — We will keep you informed.	We will keep you informed, listen to and acknowledge concerns and aspirations, and provide feedback on how public input influenced the decision.	We will work with you to ensure that your concerns and aspirations are directly reflected in the alternatives developed and provide feedback on how public input influenced the decision.	We will look to you for advice and innovation in formulating solutions and incorporate your advice and recommendations into the decisions to the maximum extent possible.	We will implement what you decide.

Source: Reprinted with the permission of IAP2.org.

Fig. 1. Spectrum of Public Participation (c) International Association for Public Participation.

certification, standards of practice, core values and advocacy. The IAP2 spectrum is a valuable guide for engaged scholarship as research indicates that more participatory methods of engagement where stakeholders can co-create solutions have the greatest transformational potential for impact (Brown et al., 2006; Butcher et al., 2011; Collins et al., 2014; Cooper & Orrell, 2016; Eatman et al., 2018; Gusheh et al., 2019; Miszczak & Patel, 2018; Palmer et al., 2020; Saltmarsh et al., 2015; Stewart & Alrutz, 2012; van Marrewijk & Dessing, 2019).

Engagement of this kind creates the potential for impact as it characterised by increased stakeholder impact on the decision. On the IAP2 spectrum, this is indicated by engagement that seeks to *involve, collaborate* or *empower* participants through the process and the outcome.

Recognising that community and stakeholder engagement, networks and external partnerships can generate significant impact – here are the top tips to ensure that your approach to engagement is both scholarly and impactful:

UNDERSTAND YOUR CONTEXT

The first place to start is to check your universities' strategic commitment to engagement articulated in strategic plans, policies, impact frameworks and toolkits. This will give you a line of sight to the value your institution places on engagement, how they define it and how your research, teaching and engagement can align to institutional goals.

Once you have established the scope of engagement in your organisation, identify how engagement is used in your discipline, noting the key methods of engagement and the kinds of issues engagement is helping to answer in your discipline. Could a different engagement method bring new insights or perspectives to the issue?

GET INSPIRED

Imitation can be the greatest form of flattery. In academia we call it replication, and the engagement space is bursting with inspiring and exciting engagement and impact stories, generously shared by practitioners from around the world. Examine freely available resources and case studies on best practice engagement that can work for your context and discipline. Check out The National Coordinating Centre for Public Engagement which is a UK-based organisation that provides a range of resources, information and case studies for the higher education sector.[1] Similarly, The Tamarack Institute and the IAP2 provide extensive resources and information suitable for the broader community context to inspire the design of your next engagement project, collaboration or partnership.[2-3]

DO A SKILLS INVENTORY

What do you know already about community and stakeholder engagement? What more do you need to know? As academics, qualitative and/or qualitative methods are at the heart of the research we conduct and the insights we seek to share with the world. However, this does not always translate into impactful engagement.

Research methodologies that include methods such as surveys or focus groups may be seeking to elicit feedback or insights from participants; however, as illustrated by the IAP2 spectrum of engagement in Fig. 1, these methods are quite low on the spectrum of engagement impact.

Additional methods or an adjustment to your methodology might be required to boost the engagement impact of your design. If you need some support with the fundamentals, consider upskilling through engagement training. An accredited

IAP2 Engagement Certificate can provide you with all the skills that you need to plan, design and evaluate your engagement programmes.[4]

GET CLEAR ON THE PURPOSE OF YOUR ENGAGEMENT, LEVEL OF IMPACT AND EVALUATION

The purpose of your engagement will help to inform the level of engagement impact and how you are going to evaluate it. Key to clarifying the purpose of your engagement is to identify the level of influence or impact the participants will have on the decision. The greater the impact, the further the purpose of engagement will sit on the IAP2 spectrum of engagement.

A Theory of Change process can help you to map out your priorities, goals and pathways for an engagement impact plan.[5] An Engagement Planning Canvas can help you pull it all together.[6] When considering evaluation, there are a range of resources that provide guidance. The IAP2 Australasia Quality Assurance Standard is one example that can help you evaluate the quality of your engagement process.[7]

BUILD YOUR NETWORK TO COLLABORATE FOR IMPACT

The social capital literature highlights the importance of building connections to individuals across broad networks as one of the key ways to get ahead. Find collaborators who share your vision for change in government, the community sector, your discipline and industry. Build the relationship through small projects or collaborations to build trust and to identify areas of shared value. Work towards establishing a Memorandum of Understanding (MOU) or a more informal partnership to advance a shared goal.

For example, the Sunshine Coast Council and University of the Sunshine Coast Regional Partnership Agreement was established for both institutions to work collaboratively to advance projects that support the social, economic and environmental interests of the Sunshine Coast region, including a project to advance excellence in community and stakeholder engagement.

Mentors are invaluable as you assemble your 'tribe' of engaged scholars. Seek out colleagues conducting impactful engagement that you admire and invite them to give you feedback on your engagement impact plan. Ask your mentor to introduce you to other engaged scholars. Join or establish a network for engaged scholarship at your institution, or an engagement Community of Practice in your broader region to grow your networks even further.

COMMUNICATE YOUR GOALS AND YOUR IMPACT

While conferences and journal articles are often a preferred mode of communicating research, communicating your findings and impact to a broader audience through online mediums can help to increase understanding of an issue, build your profile and expose you to new and exciting collaboration and partnership opportunities.

KEEP TRACK OF YOUR PROGRESS

Many engagement journeys can have intangible impacts and/ or longer-term outcomes. Keep track of your engagement processes and impact through evaluation. Make a clear link between your engagement impact plan and your teaching and research so you can build a portfolio of evidence for your next application for promotion. Finally, be reflexive in your practice – your thoughts and reflections are a powerful tool for deep learning!

DEVELOP YOUR ENGAGEMENT PRACTICE THROUGHOUT YOUR CAREER

Build your engagement expertise over the course of your career by setting an annual goal that pushes your engagement skills further along the IAP2 continuum towards engagement that empowers. This could be as simple as gradually intro-ducing more participatory and co-created methods into your engagement design to gradually build your skills, as outlined in Table 1.

While this table indicates a simple and easy way to build your skills in impactful engagement over the course of your career, it is important to note that the IAP2 spectrum is designed as a *framework* for engagement, and is not intended to be used as a linear process in the *design* of engagement.

Each engagement design will align with at least one (or two) elements that indicate the level of influence on engage-ment. For example, one phase of the engagement design may *collaborate* using the PhotoVoice method to frame the issues and identify possible solutions and could then *consult* with the community via surveys and public displays to select the preferred option.

The journey to impactful engagement, like any new skill, takes time and practice. It also requires a consistent forward momentum over the course of your career. This doesn't need to be an overwhelming proposition – goal setting and a growth mindset is important here to keep you on track.

All you need is some planning and a few short- and long-term goals, mapped to where you are now in your career and where you want to be in future. You can build a portfolio

Table 1. Building Impactful Engagement Academic Skills Throughout Your Career.

Engagement Participation Level

	Inform	Consult	Involve	Collaborate	Empower
Level of Influence					
Engagement Goal	To provide the public with balanced and objective information to assist them in understanding the problem, alternatives, opportunities and/or solutions.	To obtain public feedback on analysis, alternatives and/or decisions.	To work directly with the public throughout the process to ensure that public concerns are consistently understood and considered.	To partner with the community in each aspect of the decision, including the development of alternatives and the identification of the preferred solution.	To place final decision-making in the hands of the public.
Example of engagement Methods	• Blogs, social media articles; • Community education programme;	• Surveys; • Public display; • Public meetings/ briefings;	• Appreciative enquiry; • Community advisory Groups; • Conversation/study circles;	• Action Research; • Co-design; • Community visioning;	• Citizen's jury; • Participatory budgeting/ decision-making;

Table 1. (*Continued*)

Engagement Participation Level ↑

Level of Influence	Inform	Consult	Involve	Collaborate	Empower
	• Information Sheets/ website/webinars; • Public display/tours.	• Social media articles; • Public submissions.	• Focus groups/ interviews; • Graphic recording; • Workshops; • World café.	• Deliberative democracy processes; • Delphi processes; • Open Space processes; • PhotoVoice; • Summit.	• Participatory action Research; • Voting.

Increasing use of participatory engagement methods over your career ↑

that demonstrates the impact of your research and engagement through:

- Understanding your context

- Seek inspiration from best practice engagement examples across the world

- Do a skills inventory

- Get clear on the purpose of your engagement, level of impact and evaluation

- Build your network to collaborate for impact

- Communicate your goals and your impact

- Keep track of your progress

- Develop your engagement practice throughout your career.

Engagement has a significant role to play in bringing diverse voices and perspectives together to shape decisions and change, and in so doing, create impact. In the context of rapid and emergent global change, the need for meaningful and impactful engagement has never been more urgent.

NOTES

1. Access this resource at https://www.publicengagement.ac.uk/.
2. Access this resource at https://www.tamarackcommunity.ca/communityengagement.
3. Access IAP2 Australian website resources at https://iap2.org.au/. Note: some resources are for IAP2 members only.
4. Information about the IAP2 Australia engagement certificate training can be accessed at https://iap2.org.au/training/iap2a-certificate/.
5. An example theory of change template can be accessed at https://diytoolkit.org/tools/theory-of-change/.

6. An example engagement planning canvas template can be accessed by searching the Tamarack Resource Library at https://www.tamarackcommunity.ca/hubfs/Resources/Tools/ engagement.
7. The IAP2 Quality Assurance Standard can be accessed at https://iap2.org.au/wp-content/uploads/2019/07/ IAP2_Quality_Assurance_Standard_2015.pdf.

REFERENCES

Boyer, E. (1996). The scholarship of engagement. *Journal of Public Service and Outreach*, *1*(1), 11–20.

Brown, R. E., Reed, C. S., Bates, L. V., Knaggs, D., Casey, K. M., & Barnes, J. V. (2006). The transformative engagement process: Foundations and supports for university-community partnerships. *Journal of Higher Education Outreach and Engagement*, *11*(1), 9.

Butcher, J., Bezzina, M., & Moran, W. (2011). Transformational partnerships: A new agenda for higher education. *Innovative Higher Education*, *36*(1), 29–40. https://doi.org/10.1007/s10755-010-9155-7

Collins, C., Neal, J., & Neal, Z. (2014). Transforming individual civic engagement into community collective efficacy: The role of bonding social capital. *American Journal of Community Psychology*, *54*(3), 328–336. https://doi.org/10.1007/s10464-014-9675-x

Cooper, L., & Orrell, J. (2016). University and community engagement: Towards a partnership based on deliberate reciprocity. In F. Trede & C. McEwen (Eds.), *Educating the Deliberate Professional: Preparing for Future Practices* (Vol. 17, pp. 107–123). Springer.

Eatman, T., Saltmarsh, J., Middleton, M., & Wittman, A. (2018). Co-constructing knowledge spheres in the academy: Developing frameworks and tools for advancing publicly engaged scholarship. *Urban Education*, *53*(4), 532–561. https://doi.org/10.1177/0042085918762590

Edelman Trust Barometer. (2020). Australia: The trust ten. https://www.edelman.com.au//sites/g/files/aatuss381/files/2020-02/Edelman%20Trust%20Barometer%202020_Australian%20Key%20Findings.pdf

Edelman Trust Barometer. (2021). Global trust barometer. https://www.edelman.com/sites/g/files/aatuss191/files/2021-03/2021%20Edelman%20Trust%20Barometer.pdf

EY. (2020). Are you reframing your future or is the future reframing you? EY megatrends 2020 and beyond (3rd ed.). https://assets.ey.com/content/dam/ey-sites/ey-com/en_gl/topics/megatrends/ey-megatrends-2020-report.pdf

Gusheh, M., Firth, V., Netherton, C., & Pettigrew, C. (2019). The creation of the UTS social impact framework: A collaborative approach for transformational change. *Gateways: International Journal of Community Research and Engagement*, *12*(2). http://dx.doi.org/10.5130/ijcre.v12i2.6453

van Marrewijk, A., & Dessing, N. (2019). Negotiating reciprocal relationships: Practices of engaged scholarship in project studies. *International Journal of Project Management*, *37*(7), 884–895. https://doi.org/10.1016/j.ijproman.2019.07.001

Miszczak, S. M., & Patel, Z. (2018). The role of engaged scholarship and co-production to address urban challenges: A case study of the cape town knowledge transfer programme. *South African Geographical Journal*, *100*(2), 233–248. https://doi.org/10.1080/03736245.2017.1409649

Osborne, C., Mayo, L., & Bussey, M. (2021). New frontiers in local government community engagement: Towards transformative place-based futures. *Futures*, *131*. https://doi.org/10.1016/j.futures.2021.102768

Palmer, J., Burton, L. J., & Walsh, A. (2020). Emerging spheres of engagement: The role of trust and care in community–university research. *Qualitative Research*, 1–18. February 2020. https://doi.org/10.1177%2F1468794120904891

Saltmarsh, J., Janke, E. M., & Clayton, P. H. (2015). Transforming higher education through and for democratic civic engagement: A model for change. *Michigan Journal of Community Service Learning*, *22*(1), 122.

Stewart, T., & Alrutz, M. (2012). Meaningful relationships: Cruxes of university-community partnerships for sustainable and happy engagement. *Journal of Community Engagement and Scholarship*, *5*(1), 44–55.

Taylor, B., Walton, A., Loechel, B., Measham, T., & Fleming, D. (2017). *Strategic foresight for regional Australia: Megatrends, scenarios and implications*. Canberra, Australia.

6

KNOWLEDGE MOBILIZATION: CREATING A PATH TO IMPACT

Lauren Albrecht and Catherine Scott

ABSTRACT

Knowledge mobilization (KMb) offers an approach to conducting impactful research. In this chapter, we describe ways to remove barriers to understanding and implementing a KMb approach. We do this by examining the broad scope of KMb, thinking about how it has evolved over time, and focusing on core intent rather than terminology debates. Our goal is to offer a pragmatic series of stepping stones that form a KMb pathway. These steps include: (1) asking good questions; (2) aligning your work with what has already been done; (3) acquiring new and diverse knowledge; (4) adapting knowledge to a specific context; (5) applying knowledge in the real world; and (6) assessing what works and what doesn't throughout your journey. We argue that this process will identify and support successful implementation of nuanced, novel, and meaningful solutions to real-world problems. Following the KMb pathway will guide you toward becoming an impactful academic who creates a lasting research legacy and a positive mark on the world.

Keywords: Knowledge mobilization; knowledge translation; knowledge transfer and exchange; knowledge to action; evidence-informed practice; community-engaged research

INTRODUCTION

Previous chapters have emphasized the value of identifying your desired impact, followed by connecting and leveraging supports (i.e., institutional, academic, community, and industry) to achieve your goals. Creating new relationships and finding new resources are important activities as you grow in your career; however, it is equally important to nourish your existing connections, for connection is what lies at the heart of knowledge mobilization (KMb). Connecting different sources of information together to understand what is known and connecting people with this ever-emerging evidence and leading practices to guide growth and development.

In this chapter, we explore the question, "why is knowledge mobilization vital to achieving impact?" To answer this question, we will clarify the meaning of KMb. Our aim is to strip away the debates on terminology that delay action and instead focus on intent, essential elements, and underlying theory to guide KMb practice. In doing so, we will illustrate how the elements of KMb are like stepping stones that can create an effective path to impact across often quickly moving and sometimes murky waters. We will examine key considerations at each stepping stone to understand how they may be interconnected and think about the ripple effects of our philosophical approach and research choices along the way. Our hope is that by the end of this chapter, you will feel prepared to choose KMb approaches that align with your research methods, your career goals, and ultimately your desired impact. This process highlights that in KMb, as in life, there is no one right path to become an impactful academic.

CONNECTING KMB WITH RESEARCH IMPACT

Despite the massive volume of research published over the last 30 years, examples of direct application of this evidence in policy and practice are relatively few. Understanding why it's difficult to apply research evidence is fundamental to adopting more effective strategies to use what we know (or KMb) to achieve positive change (or impact).

Historically, research evidence and knowledge were conflated, which limited our ability to influence change. To illustrate this conundrum, think about a recent decision that you've made (e.g., accepting a new job, going back to school, taking a course, making a decision about your health and well-being). What influenced your decision? Did you use research evidence, or did other things influence your decision (e.g., the opinion of your peers, values, available resources, previous experience, etc.)? When we think about it this way, it is clear that research evidence on its own is rarely sufficient to influence decision-making, let alone policy and practice changes. Decision-making processes are highly contextualized and necessarily take many sources of evidence into account (e.g., experiential, contextual, historical). It is for this reason that we prefer to use the term evidence-informed practice rather than evidence-based practice, as decisions are rarely based on research evidence alone.

Defining what we mean by evidence, knowledge, and knowledge mobilization sets the stage for why KMb is important and how we can practically apply what we know to achieve impact. Data are a collection of facts, which become information once they are processed and organized in some way (Dammann, 2018). Evidence is information that has been assessed for credibility. Knowledge is generated when information and evidence are used or applied to achieve an end, and wisdom is gained from the process of applying knowledge.

UNDERSTANDING KMB WHAT IT IS AND WHAT IT ISN'T

Around the globe and across disciplines, many terms are used to refer to KMb (Bragge, 2017; Crocket, 2019; Graham, 2006). For example, in the Canadian health sciences, knowledge translation is the preferred term; however, knowledge mobilization is preferred in the Canadian social sciences. Rather than make a ruling on the correct wording, our aim is to focus on the overall unifying intent: to use knowledge to improve society (KMb Toolkit, 2019). How we define and measure these social improvements then leads us to impact.

When thinking about how to practically engage in KMb, it's important to delineate what KMb is and isn't. KMb can be described as an ongoing commitment to learning and applying knowledge to solving real-life problems (KMb Toolkit, 2019). KMb is not necessarily training or a specific credential, nor is it solely focused on communications, marketing, or networking. All these skills are relevant to KMb and can be part of a robust KMb approach, but they are not sufficient, in and of themselves. The aim of KMb is to cocreate knowledge that informs contextually relevant decisions and action.

THE EVOLUTION OF KMB

KMb has evolved over the years in ways that have mirrored the evolution of science more broadly. Based on an understanding of science as uncovering universal truths and evidence being conflated with knowledge, KMb, at its earliest conceptions, was focused on the pursuit of identifying "best practices" that transcended context. As the limitations of this approach were increasingly recognized, KMb shifted toward embracing complexity, rather than removing it, by examining the use of knowledge in context. This is based on a more nuanced understanding of the "real-world" and an understanding of knowledge as being socially constructed.

HONING IN ON KMB

Just as there are many terms that are broadly interchangeable with KMb, there are even more associated models to guide your KMb practice. These include:

- Diffusion of Innovation Theory (Greenhalgh et al., 2005; Rogers, 2003)

- Donabedian Model (Donabedian, 1988)

- PARiHS Framework (Kitson et al., 1998)

- Practice Guidelines Evaluation and Adaptation Cycle (Graham & Harrison, 2005)

- The Knowledge-to-Action Framework (Graham et al., 2006)

- ADAPTE process (Fervers et al., 2011)

- CAN-IMPLEMENT (Harrison et al., 2013)

- AIMD (Bragge et al., 2017)

Models can act as a guide to augment and streamline your approach for developing and implementing a KMb plan; however, they can also limit your field of view. We recommend that you examine and learn from these models and theoretical perspectives, but also that you stay open to the possibility of adapting them to your particular context. Getting locked into one way of doing things is antithetical to robust KMb practice and may unintentionally limit the potential for adoption and use of research.

To help you to stay open and flexible, we have extracted several essential elements from across the various models and frameworks. These core elements can act as stepping stones, creating a KMb pathway with the goal of linking knowledge to social impact through the research process (Fig. 1). What follows is a description of these core components and the key

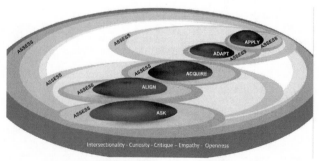

Fig. 1. KMb Stepping Stones.

considerations at each step to help develop and implement a KMb plan. Exploring each stepping stone and making decisions about how to approach them in context will support you to build the knowledge and skills needed to embrace KMb as part of your day-to-day research practice. We call this moving from KMb awareness toward KMb commitment.

Stepping Stone One – Ask: Good Questions Are Critical

Questions are foundational to research as they become the lens through which everything that follows is viewed. If the framing of your questions are flawed or biased, that thinking will be baked into all subsequent actions. For example, if you create a question based on an assumed knowledge gap without first confirming the parameters of that gap, you may spend several weeks, if not months, developing a project that does not contribute to the knowledge base.

Asking good questions may start with you, but it doesn't end with you. As a researcher, it's critical to explore and pursue your curiosities, but an impactful academic seeks out new knowledge, particularly from differing perspectives, to develop and hone their research questions. Reflexive research practice means gathering these data before you establish your questions and then using this knowledge to locate and examine your biases.

It's not always a straightforward or easy process, but you can think of it in the following formula (Fig. 2):

Fig. 2. Adapted From Maxwell, 2005 – An Interactive Model of Research Design.

To truly apply this formula to the development of your research questions, you will most likely need to engage with others who have a stake in this issue (Step 2) and acquire knowledge about this issue from multiple sources (Step 3). Think of this process as a minifeedback loop that brings rich understanding to your work. Once you have engaged in this cycle of reading, thinking, asking, listening, learning, and reflecting, you will have the tools needed to develop robust questions. From there, your questions will determine the best methodologies and methods to apply for seeking answers.

Stepping Stone Two – Align: Work With Others Who Have a Stake in This Issue

It is a simple truism – KMb cannot occur without collaboration. It is imperative to identify and build relationships with others who have experience with and a stake in the problems you are seeking to address. Each collaborator brings epistemic advantage based on their unique positionality (i.e., citizen, patient, researcher, clinician). Engaging with these vantage points is essential to effectively understanding and addressing the issue at hand.

Some academics have expressed fear that by incorporating multiple voices, it will "water down" the objectivity and objectives of the research. This fear is rooted in a paradigm of science as the process of discovering "the truth." By engaging with multiple voices, research shifts from being conducted *on passive subjects* toward being conducted *with active participants*. The former is highly engrained in traditional views of science and the ways in which we learn to be academics, but research has shown how much more effective the latter is. This shift can feel daunting, but to truly dismantle power dynamics, researchers need to be vulnerable and open with collaborators. Resist temptation to avoid this discomfort by reverting to the old model of science. The saying "you don't know what you don't know" has variably been attributed to Socrates, Plato, and Aristotle. Whatever its origins, the intent is to encourage you to approach collaborators with curiosity so that you can discover what is important to them and the challenges they face.

When working with others, there are certain ethical obligations in KMb that must be fully considered at the outset. By drawing others into your work, there is an obligation to provide return on investment and work toward codefining research questions, processes, and outcomes. This means that when you are defining impact through a KMb lens, you as the researcher can't be the only one to decide what the desired impact should be. It is also critical to share with stakeholders and communities what has been learned in ways that meet the needs of communities. It is important that all parties gain meaningful knowledge – not just the researcher, the funder, and the potential publishers.

Stepping Stone Three – Acquire: Gather Knowledge From Multiple Sources

Making an impactful contribution to research means building on what is already known. To do this, a comprehensive understanding is needed of that which has come before. This includes knowledge that has been captured in publications from a variety of research designs, not just systematic reviews, meta-analyses, or randomized controlled trials. Examining qualitative research and sources of knowledge outside of academic journals (e.g., case studies, organizational or governmental reports, websites, blog posts) can be rich sources of context and in-depth understanding of an issue. Be wary of the evidence hierarchy or the tendency to privilege specific forms of evidence based on disciplinary biases.

Consider the volume of traditionally published knowledge – there are millions of available studies to learn from. Don't reinvent the wheel! Search, read, identify what you can use, and flag gaps you might need to fill. Don't limit yourself to works only from within your discipline – explore outside of your silos. For example, you will find robust literature about partnerships across several disciplines, and each brings forward their own understandings and approaches (e.g., health services, sociology, management, law, social work, psychology, education).

Many valuable insights do not make it past the proverbial cutting room floor and remain unpublished. Searching outside of traditional publications (often referred to as the grey literature) is critical to tapping into this vast resource. But nothing beats talking to people! Developing strategies and skills for learning from the experience of people – both academic and nonacademic – is as important as your skills in reading, reviewing, and critically appraising the research literature.

Stepping Stone Four – Adapt: Make Meaning of Knowledge in Context

While we may sound like a broken record, it holds true – the work of KMb cannot be done alone. Researchers cannot know all contexts intimately. Context experts (i.e., people that live and work in the setting of interest) are essential partners when adapting knowledge for specific research purposes.

As partners, context experts have valuable insights on more than just the population or environment of focus. Soliciting their thoughts on processes, methods, and interpretation will strengthen the adaptation process. Questions to explore with them could include:

- Does the knowledge that you bring to bear about the project resonate with their experience? What are your knowledge gaps?

- Is this the right time for this project?

- Are there upcoming events that could hinder or facilitate the project?

- Is there a time when people are too busy to engage with research and a time when it is better to make connections?

- Who will own the data? Where will data be held?

- Is there a culturally appropriate way to create connections?

- Has there been past traumatic experiences with research?

- Are there methods of data collection that are more suitable and acceptable?

- How should the end products of the research be shared back?

Working with context experts also reveals the influences from micro-, meso-, and macrosystems within the context of your study. Engaging with partners who have contextual knowledge throughout design and implementation phases of research will uncover how exo-systems, such as government, regulatory bodies, economic systems, and media, influence local attitudes and actions.

An understanding of context is absolutely essential so that your research does not ignore or perpetuate systems of oppression. It is critical that relationships with context experts and research participants are built upon an anti-oppressive lens. Antioppressive approaches acknowledge and address privilege, power, and intersectionality; critical components of antioppressive practices include antiracism, antisexism, anti-heterosexism, antiableism, antiageism, and class oppression (Moore, 2003). This thinking must infuse all aspects of the research continuum. If understanding how to approach these concepts within your research plan is challenging, this is an excellent opportunity for identifying collaborators who can bring this lens.

Incorporating antioppressive practices is not only a leading practice, but is often a requirement of research. Most universities and ethics review bodies require commitments to antioppressive research practices in order to receive research approvals. For example, when working with First Nations communities in Canada, training related to the First Nations Principles of OCAP ® (Ownership Control Access Possession) (FNIGC, 2021) is a requirement for funding. Similarly, the gender-based analysis plus (GBA+, 2021) policy and research tool is strongly recommended, if not required, to receive project funding through Canadian government programs. The GBA+ tool helps to identify who benefits and who is excluded from organizational decisions. If antioppressive practices are unfamiliar or new to you, explore professional development opportunities at your institution or within your region and seek out collaborators that can bring this lens to your work.

Stepping Stone Five – Apply: Move From Knowledge to Real-World Practice

Applying knowledge in context is not for the faint of heart, but this is where there is great potential to see direct impact from research. This stage requires an extensive understanding of the underlying principles of change management, organizational change, and implementation science. While these are entire fields of work in their own right, a few key messages can guide you in on your KMb journey; we encourage you to delve more deeply into these bodies of literature as you progress.

Applying knowledge is often done to create or facilitate a change; but, just the word "change" can be enough to drive people away. However, if framed as improvement, you may find a more receptive audience. Essential stages of change to facilitate knowledge application can be found across many change management models (e.g., ADKAR ®, Kotter's eight step change model ®), including:

- awareness of the need for change;

- motivation or desire to change and creating a sense of urgency to change;

- connecting with people who will guide the change, creating and communicating a vision for change, acquiring information and knowledge to inform changes in behavior, structures, and processes;

- implementing change or taking action and learning as you go, and;

- strategies that reinforce and reward behavior and ongoing improvement.

                                    (Hiatt, 2006; Kotter, 2007)

Individual-level change and organizational-level change are linked, but by its very nature, organizational change requires more focus on collaboration. Collaboration requires more than just being in the same room at the same time, there must also be agreement on the need for change, joint planning, concrete and sequenced organization-wide strategies for implementing change, as well as mechanisms for ongoing organizational learning and improvement. If your project is intended to have an impact at the organizational-level, plan for the significant time and resources needed to meaningfully influence change at this level.

Applying knowledge can also take the form of implementing a "thing." This "thing" can be a practice, process, intervention, or innovation. The process of implementing something uses expertise from the business fields of change management and organizational change. Successful implementation efforts require flexibility and tolerance for ambiguity as plans evolve in the real world. Build in strategies to support learning, unlearning, and relearning along the way (Collison & Parcell, 2004). Know that you will need to negotiate and prioritize the actions you take in collaboration with people who have context and content expertise. A researcher is not a soloist; rather, implementation is akin to a symphony performance. There are many instruments with different and layered parts, and the beautiful music comes from putting them all together in a planned and practiced manner.

Unfortunately, much of the "secret sauce" of knowledge application, change, and implementation isn't ultimately published. As a result, it is extremely important to seek out grey literature from different disciplines and learn alongside people who have done this type of work before. This is another instance of not recreating the wheel! When you are planning, make sure that you look to those who have done this before and gather the expertise needed from different disciplines to help you navigate the bumps in the road because there will be many!

Stepping Stone Ripples – Assess: Understand What Works and What Doesn't and Adjust Along the Way

To understand whether your KMb journey have been effective, it is essential to assess what's working, what is not, and course-correct throughout to achieve your research goals. Thinking about it this way, assessment is less of a stepping stone and more like ripples around each stepping stone on your KMb journey. It's important to look beyond the typical research endpoint (i.e., predefined hypothesis or primary outcome) and to be curious about all aspects of the research and KMb journey – including examining processes as well as intended and unintended outcomes. Key questions can help you to formulate indicators to assess, such as:

How Do You and Your Collaborators Define Success?

This means understanding what is meaningful from all perspectives and prioritizing the indicators of success that are most relevant to your collaborative research and impact goals (Gugerty & Karlan, 2018). For example, traditional indicators of success include the number and quality of publications and number and dollar value of grants received; however, these are very specific indicators of value to one particular audience. Understanding what's important to your collaborators will expand these indicators; for example, collaborators may be interested in policy or process changes among others.

How Will You Track Progress Toward Your Goals?

Consider using a Theory of Change or program logic model to define inputs, actions, outputs, and short-, medium-, and long-term outcomes. Remember that process outcomes are as important as summative outcomes, especially if your research doesn't generate the results you expected. This means examining how something was done to achieve the endpoint and thinking through both the intended and unintended effects of this process. Tools like After Action Reviews and Retrospectives (Collison & Parcell, 2004) can also support iterative cycles of learning and improvement to identify "lessons learned" and support small changes along the way that can ultimately have a significant influence on your work.

How Will You Critically Appraise Evidence Generated Through Your Research?

Given the complexity of assessing impact, be wary of getting locked into traditional hierarchical assessments of evidence. Rather, consider evidence "fit for purpose". For example, during the COVID-19 pandemic, random controlled trials (RCTs) provided critical evidence to assess the efficacy and effectiveness of vaccines. However, RCTs can't provide evidence to help us understand vaccine hesitancy or engage in science communication to support people to change their attitudes toward vaccinations. This example emphasizes the importance of gaining familiarity with a range of approaches to appraising different evidence sources.

ARRIVING AT THE OTHER END? THE JOURNEY IS NEVER COMPLETE

These stepping stones are not offered to you as a one-and-done path or process for success. Effective and impactful KMb is a mission that is never complete. Engaging in these steps again (and again) is an iterative process of continuous learning. There is always more to learn in service of solving real-world problems because the world is constantly in flux.

This continuous cycle of gaining and applying knowledge has been illustrated in different models (Harrison & Graham, 2021). Regardless of the model you use, reflecting and learning from both successes and challenges in the research process, the relationships you create, the contexts you operate in, and the processes you have used will generate new knowledge that you can apply in your next project.

To leverage the KMb pathway in your journey to become an impactful academic, it is important to remain curious, open, empathetic, critical of grand truths devoid of context, and intersectional in your approaches. These are the humble waters that are foundational to this approach. To do this means decentering the traditional mission of academia to claim expertise and acknowledge the limits of personal knowledge, seek out opportunities to see the world beyond ourselves, and share the power to make decisions about the questions that are asked, how they are answered, and the ways in which data are interpreted.

KNOWING THE CHALLENGES THAT LAY AHEAD

KMb is new(ish) to academia, so it is not yet fully integrated into the traditional academic reward scheme. According to a 2018 Canadian survey examining Social Sciences and Humanities Research Council–funded education researchers, minimal university supports are offered toward KMb efforts (Cooper et al., 2018). It was also noted that where supports did exist, they were not well accessed by researchers (Cooper et al., 2018).

The lack of institutional support and lack of awareness of the few existing supports is especially challenging for new academics seeking promotion and tenure. Good KMb takes time and significant effort to establish and maintain meaningful relationships with nonacademic audiences. Lack of dedicated funding for these efforts and short-term research funding cycles can make this a challenging investment when time is at a premium. The publication imperative and the hierarchy of preferred publication types and venues can be an additional hurdle toward this commitment early in an academic career. But take heart, there is a robust scientific discipline devoted to examining "what works, for whom, and in what context" that you can draw from and publish within. This includes journals like *Implementation Science*, *Implementation Science Communications*, and *Action Research*. Explore these resources and contribute to the knowledge therein, but don't forget to find other ways to democratize the knowledge you have gained by engaging in approaches to KMb that are not hidden behind paywalls and written in academic jargon. Remember, impact is generated when what we have learned is shared, applied, and adopted!

GO FORTH AND BE IMPACTFUL

The current social reality is that academia can no longer remain apart from society. Governments cannot continue to justify public funding for projects that do not benefit citizens broadly. With limited research funds available, return on investment is of increasing importance. KMb offers opportunities to conduct better, more socially just science because the intent is to change an old model of academic practice and meaningfully incorporate "the other" into the research process. By seeking out and actively engaging others with a stake in real-world problems in the problem identification and problem-solving process, the solutions you come to will be nuanced, novel, and meaningful.

KMb also helps to broaden the long-term potential of your academic work. It creates opportunities for sustained relationships, engagements, and partnerships that can grow and evolve alongside your research program. Through this openness to learning, relearning, and growth, different types of publications become possible, including exploration of methods, KMb processes, KMb practices, lessons learned, negative or null studies, process evaluations, and effectiveness studies focused on short-, medium-, and long-term outcomes. It is without question that KMb offers a robust path to becoming an impactful academic that creates a lasting research legacy and a positive mark on the world. So go forth and be impactful!

Resources to Extend Your Knowledge

- Critical Examination of Knowledge to Action Models and Implications for Promoting Health Equity.

Link: https://nccdh.ca/images/uploads/KT_Model_EN.pdf

- Knowledge Translation: The Rise of Implementation

Link: https://ktdrr.org/products/kt-implementation/KT-Implementation-508.pdf

- Guidelines for Effective Knowledge Mobilization from the Social Sciences and Humanities Research Council

Link: https://www.sshrc-crsh.gc.ca/funding-financement/
policies-politiques/knowledge_mobilisation-mobilisation_
des_connaissances-eng.aspx

- Questing Your Way to a Knowledge Mobilization Strategy:
Doing research that is useful and used

Link: https://carleton.ca/communityfirst/wp-content/uploads/
KMB-Questing-Your-Way-to-a-KMb-Strategy-Jun-29-
2015.pdf

- Imagining the Future of Knowledge Mobilization: Perspectives from UNESCO Chairs

Link: https://research-groups.usask.ca/unesco-biocultural/
images/imaginingfutureofknowledgemobilization.pdf

- The Registry of Methods and Tools for Organizational
Change

Link: https://www.nccmt.ca/organizational-change

- KMb Toolkit covers planning, doing and evaluating KMb

Link: http://www.kmbtoolkit.ca/

- Knowledge Translation Training and Resources

Link: https://www.sickkids.ca/en/learning/continuing-profes-
sional-development/knowledge-translation-training/

- Knowledge Mobilisation Research resources compiled by
the National Institute for Health Research

Link: https://www.nihr.ac.uk/documents/knowledge-mobi-
lisation-research/22598

• Research Impact Canada's KMb Journal Club

Link: https://researchimpact.ca/category/kmb-journal-club/

• Core Knowledge Translation Competencies: A Scoping Review

Link: https://bmchealthservres.biomedcentral.com/articles/10.1186/s12913-018-3314-4

REFERENCES

Bragge, P., Grimshaw, J. M., Lokker, C., Colquhoun, H., & The AIMD Writing/Working Group. (2017). AIMD – A validated, simplified framework of interventions to promote and integrate evidence into health practices, systems, and policies. *BMC Medical Research Methodology, 17*, 3. https://doi.org/10.1186/s12874-017-0314-8

Collison, C., & Parcell, G. (2004). *Learning to fly: Practical knowledge management from leading and learning organizations.* Capstone Publishing Ltd.

Cooper, A., Rodway, J., & Read, R. (2018). Knowledge mobilization practices of educational researchers across Canada. *Canadian Journal of Higher Education, 48*(1). https://doi.org/10.47678/cjhe.v48i1.187983

Crockett, L. (2019). What's in a name? Knowledge translation nomenclature. https://medium.com/knowledgenudge/kt-lingo-101-131983b06f5c

Dammann, O. (2018). Data, information, evidence, and knowledge: A proposal for health informatices and data science. *Online Journal of Public Health Informatics*, *10*(3), e224. https://doi.org/10.5210/ojphi.v10i3.9631

Donabedian, A. (1988). The quality of care: How can it be assessed? *JAMA*, *260*(12), 1743–1748. https://doi.org/10.1001/jama.1988.03410120089033

Fervers, B., Burgers, J. S., Voellinger, R., Brouwers, M., Browman, G. P., Graham, I. D., Harrison, M. B., Latreille, J., Mlika-Cabane, N., Paquet, L., Zitzelsberger, L., & Burnand, B., & ADAPTE Collaboration. (2011). Guideline adaptation: An approach to enhance efficiency in guideline development and improve utilisation. *BMJ Quality and Safety*, *20*(3), 228–236. https://doi.org/10.1136/bmjqs.2010.043257. Epub 2011 Jan 5. PMID: .21209134.

FNIGC. (2021). *First Nations principles of ownership, Control, access, possession.* First Nations Information Governance Centre. Retrieved from the internet. https://fnigc.ca/ocap-training/. Accessed on November 15, 2021.

GBA+. (2021). *Gender-based analysis plus.* Government of Canada. Retrieved from the internet. https://women-gender-equality.canada.ca/en/gender-based-analysis-plus.html. Accessed on November 15, 2021.

Graham, I. D., & Harrison, M. B. (2005). Evaluation and adaptation of clinical practice guidelines. *Evidence-Based Nursing*, *8*, 68–72.

Graham, I. D., Logan, J., Harrison, M. B., Straus, S. E., Tetroe, J., Caswell, W., & Robinson, N. (2006). Lost in knowledge translation: Time for a map? *Journal of Continuing Education in the Health Professions.* Winter, *26*(1), 13–24. https://doi.org/10.1002/chp.47. PMID: 16557505.

Greenhalgh, T., Robert, G., Bate, P., acfarlane, F., & Kyriakidou, O. (2005). *Diffusion of innovations in health service organizations: A systematic review of the literature.* Blackwell Publishing Ltd.

Gugerty, M. K., & Karlan, D. (2018). Ten reasons not to measure impact and what to do instead. *Stanford Social Innovation Review.* https://ssir.org/articles/entry/ten_reasons_not_to_measure_impact_and_what_to_do_instead

Harrison, M. B., & Graham, I. D. (2021). *Knowledge translation in nursing and healthcare: A roadmap to evidence-informed practice.* Wiley-Blackwell.

Harrison, M. B., Graham, I. D., van den Hoek, J., Dogherty, E. J., Carley, M. E., & Angus, V. (2013). Guideline adaptation and implementation planning: A prospective observational study. *Implementation Science, 8*, 49. https://doi.org/10.1186/1748-5908-8-49

Hiatt, J. M. (2006). *ADKAR: A model for change in business, government, and our community.* Prosci Research. https://www.prosci.com/methodology/adkar

Kitson, A., Harvey, G., & McCormack, B. (1998). Enabling the implementation of evidence based practice: A conceptutal framework. *Quality in Health Care, 7*, 149–158. http://doi.org/10.116/qshc.7.3.149

KMb Toolkit. (2019). What is knowledge mobilization? http://www.kmbtoolkit.ca/what-is-kmb

Kotter, J. P. (2007). *Leading change: Why transformation efforts fail.* Harvard Business Review.

Maxwell, J. A. (2005). *Qualitative research design: An interactive approach* (2nd ed.). Sage Publications.

Moore, P. (2003). Critical components of an anti-oppressive framework. https://cyc-net.org/cyc-online/cycol-1203-moore.html

Rogers, EM. (2003). *Diffusion of innovations* (5th ed.). Free Press. https://sphweb.bumc.bu.edu/otlt/mph-modules/sb/behavioralchangetheories/behavioralchangetheories4.html

7

DEMONSTRATING IMPACT – CONSIDERATIONS FOR COLLECTING AND COMMUNICATING THE EVIDENCE OF IMPACT

David Phipps, Anneliese Poetz and Michael Johnny

ABSTRACT

This chapter addresses one of the most challenging aspects of impact, 'how do I demonstrate that I've had an impact?' When the topic of impact comes up, researchers want to know how they'll measure it. As not all evidence is a measurement, this chapter describes how researchers can be strategic and intentional about collecting and reporting impact evidence. As discussed in Chapter 1, a narrative approach to reporting on impact is generally used and making a case compelling is achieved with compelling evidence. Drawing on learnings from previous chapters around working with stakeholders and university systems and supports, the chapter challenges the reader to consider how they might build a compelling impact case study and provides a tool to support collecting and communicating the evidence of impact of your research. Case studies are generally utilised to demonstrate different types of evidence from various disciplines, and a template is provided for researchers to begin mapping out their impact evidence plan. Consistent with the approach of the book, it is emphasised that collecting the evidence of impact is not done in isolation or for one project and then forgotten. Rather, it is a whole career approach that is aligned with an individual philosophy of academic responsibility and identity. Being able to use excellent evidence to articulate the impact your research has generated will position the researcher to better attract additional funding to generate bigger impact in the future.

Keywords: Research impact; knowledge mobilisation; impact assessment; Research Impact Canada; evidencing impact; reporting impact

WHY COLLECT AND COMMUNICATE THE EVIDENCE OF IMPACT?

Dear Researcher, let's get something correct right off the top. We are not going to ask you to measure the impact of your research. Measurement implies a quantitative method (i.e. measuring tape), and we know from Jonathan Grant's work that the case study or narrative is an appropriate unit of assessment (King's College London and Digital Science, 2015). We will not even ask you to assess your impact because an assessment implies a comparison between yours and someone else's impact. That's what happens in assessment-driven systems of research impact such as the UK where the impact discourse is dominated by the Research Excellence Framework (REF) and where a subsequent 'Impact

Agenda' has arisen (Smith et al., 2020). In countries without an assessment system, like Canada, research impact is driven by the mission of the funder, the research institution and/or the personal mission of the researcher. That's why we suggest you collect and communicate the evidence of impact arising from your research. This might be done for an individual research project but it might also be done reflecting upon a research career.

Let's be clear about something else: it is not the Wild West. You will read in the academic literature that there is little agreement on how to collect and communicate the evidence of impact. A lot has been written on impact, citing impact frameworks and evaluations (Cruz Rivera et al., 2017). While there is no consensus, we should not expect that one tool will rule them all because the context of each research to impact project is almost always different. Recall that of the 6,975 impact case studies in the 2014 REF; there were 3,709 different pathways for impact (King's, 2015). However, beyond the scholarly literature, where there is little agreement, there are practices and tools that can help you collect and communicate the evidence of impact.

One open access collection of practices is hosted by the International School on Research Impact Assessment (https://www.theinternationalschoolonria.com/). Reflecting on their many years of capacity building for research impact assessment (their words, not ours) Adam and colleagues (Adam et al., 2018, p.1) created a ten-point guideline 'which relate to (1) context, (2) purpose, (3) stakeholders' needs, (4) stakeholder engagement, (5) conceptual frameworks, (6) methods and data sources, (7) indicators and metrics, (8) ethics and conflicts of interest, (9) communication, and (10) community of practice'.

That's great for collecting the evidence of impact, but to support impact throughout your career, you need to tell people about the impact your research has had. You must both *collect and communicate the evidence of impact*. Well that's where Research Impact Canada (RIC, www.research-impact.ca) can help.

As of early 2021, RIC is a network of 21 universities with a vision of being a globally leading network that enables researchers and their partners to demonstrate contribution to, and impact of, research excellence. While we can evaluate the activities of the Network (MacGregor & Phipps, 2020), we strive to progress our vision and help demonstrate the impact of research arising from researchers at RIC member universities.

In the summer of 2016, the RIC Evaluation Committee undertook a literature review and environmental scan of different international research impact assessment systems. We landed on the REF as a starting point mainly because it was then, and remains, a standard of comparison for other national research impact assessment systems (Wróblewska, 2021). The REF guidelines tell you what counts as evidence of impact. They tell you how to communicate it by providing a case study template, but they don't tell you how to collect this evidence. The RIC tool fills this gap.

COMMUNICATING THE EVIDENCE OF IMPACT – RIC CASE STUDY TEMPLATE

We felt the REF 2014 template was too researcher and university focused. It required the researcher to speak about the impact their research made yet non-academic stakeholders are always involved in making impact happen (Phipps et al., 2016). Since stakeholders are the ones either making the impact or benefitting from the impact, the RIC case study template requires you talk to the stakeholders involved in your research and collect not only their testimonials but also the documents which corroborate the impact. These might include public minutes of meetings such as a municipal committee, meetings of a board of directors, an annual report, a legal brief or a clinical practice guideline. These are examples of documents that reference you and/or your research and can substantiate the testimonials. Rather than asking the researcher to speak for the non-academic stakeholder, the RIC tool requires you to speak to them and capture their experiences and observations of impact in their voices and in their documents. And the draft case study is always shared back to the interviewees to ensure their perspectives are captured accurately.

The RIC tool has a broad definition of research and/or expertise. This can include unpublished research made accessible by the researcher sitting on a community board or serving on a government panel. Because Canada does not have a system-wide impact assessment scheme such as REF, researchers can be more liberal with the types of research we consider eligible by including a researcher's expertise as well as their published research. Researchers are well advised to become thoroughly acquainted with the definition of impact being used in your context. While the Engagement and Impact Assessment run by the Australian Research Council may have very strict definitions of impact, a philanthropic grant may have a more generous understanding of impact.

Are you expected just to call up a stakeholder and say, 'Hey, remember me and my research? Please tell me what you did with it'. Well, you could do that, but you would get a stream of consciousness that would be hard to organise into case study with largely anecdotal evidence. Hence, we have generated a tool that will help you systematically gather the evidence of impact.

COLLECTING THE EVIDENCE OF IMPACT – RIC INTERVIEW GUIDE

A gap in the REF 2014 guidance was the lack of connection between the extensive guidance and the case study framework. The guidance provided the rules – what counted as research, what counted as impact and what counted as evidence of impact. The case study provided the format of presentation, but there was no support on how to actually collect the evidence of impact. We turned to contribution analysis (CA) to inform the development of a semi-structured interview guide because it moves impact assessment from being focused on attribution (i.e. how much of the impact can one attribute to the original research) to a focus on contribution (i.e. how did the research – in context of associated and subsequent processes and activities – contribute to the impact) (Greenhalgh, 2016).

Aligning with the Co-Produced Pathway to Impact (Phipps et al., 2016), CA (Riley et al., 2018) is based on a logic model and its application involves six steps:

1. identifying the attribution problem to be addressed

2. developing a theory of change (TOC)

3. gathering evidence on the TOC

4. assembling evidence and assessing the contribution story

5. applying an iterative process of seeking additional evidence

6. revising and strengthening the contribution story

A further convergence of CA with the Co-Produced Pathway to Impact was developed by Sarah Morton (Morton, 2015) as she aligns different stages in CA with 'research uptake', 'research use' and 'research impact' similar to 'uptake', 'implementation' and 'impact' in the co-produced pathway to impact. She presents seven stages of evaluation criteria which we turned into the start of a semi-structured interview guide.

After a few iterations with stakeholders, we generated the final version of the interview guide.[1] We used the tool (guidelines, interview guide, case study template) to create a case study of the impact of an early intervention called Hand in Hand Screening and Intervention for children with Fetal Alcohol Spectrum Disorders (FASD). Hand in Hand is a programme developed by researchers at the Infant Mental Health Promotion at the Hospital for Sick Children (Toronto, Canada) and supported in part by Kids Brain Health Network (KBHN).[2] Anneliese Poetz, then Manager of Knowledge Translation at KBHN, describes her use of the tool that she adapted to suit her needs. Here she reflects on her use of the tool, not about the case study per se.

KBHN/HAND IN HAND SCREENING AND INTERVENTION – ANNELIESE'S REFLECTIONS

The interview question about the history of the project usually was the most fruitful because it would lead them to tell the story about the present state of the project (after explaining the past), and often they'd start talking about the outcomes/impacts the project was already having. The other questions helped to gain evidence about how sustainable they felt these changes could be, which usually resulted in some good insights for creating a path forward to longer-term and broader impacts.

In addition to adapting some of the questions to my specific context, flexibility as an interviewer also came in handy in terms of the order the questions were asked. While they were ordered under specific topic headings, having the skill to fluidly jump around the interview guide/questions was essential in order not to interrupt the flow of the conversation. It helps if the interviewer can listen without interrupting the interviewee, silently crossing off any questions in the interview guide as they are being answered. Using this 'semi-structured' approach, I found it beneficial to go with where the person was taking the conversation, while jotting down probing questions as necessary.

The only feedback I received from stakeholders about the RIC tool was based on the last question (which I always ask as a qualitative researcher), 'is there anything else you would like to add?' Most, if not all interviewees said they had nothing further to add since they said I had asked them all the right questions. To me, this was a validation that the tool is sufficiently comprehensive.

Anneliese eventually produced a six-page (approx. 3,500 word) case study that was validated by the interview subjects and provided to KBHN as an official impact case study. Anneliese's account of her use and adaptation of the RIC tool illustrates how it is a tool to be adapted, not a template to be used rigidly. It is meant to be adapted to each unique context and even adapted on the fly as the interviewer listens to the interviewee and adjusts from one question to the next.

COLLECTING AND COMMUNICATING THE
EVIDENCE OF IMPACT THROUGHOUT YOUR CAREER

Now that you have seen and read Anneliese's reflections on her use of the tool, we suggest there are three ways you can use it. Two are in the context of your research project as it unfolds. The third is based on your career of 'research to impact' projects.

Project Perspective

1. Retrospectively

   • Anneliese used the tool to collect and communicate the evidence of impact on a project that had already demonstrated impact on practice and for kids and families living with FASD. This project had been part of KBHN's research portfolio for over 10 years, so it was in a mature phase. Although impact of this nature is unlikely to be obtained during the 3–5 years of your funded research grant, you can still use this tool prospectively during this phase (see below).

2. Prospectively

   • The semi-structured interview guide questions are based on a logic model, so they can be used prospectively to capture the evidence of collaboration and engagement even before any changes in policy or practice has occurred. The first two or three questions (history, responsibility, awareness) should be asked of project stakeholders right from the beginning of your research project, almost like a baseline, so you can see the evolution of engagement and impact over time. Using the tool annually throughout the term of your funded grant project will capture the evidence of ongoing engagement and collaboration, setting the stage for you to collect the evidence of impact if/when that occurs in the future.

Career Perspective

- You find yourself at the enviable position of being in a mature stage of your career. You can look back on your CV, which is now many inches thick, but does it tell the story of the societal impacts of all those publications, grad students, conference presentations, public engagement, media releases? In addition to the two project-based uses above, you can also use the RIC tool retrospectively to collect the evidence of impact over your career. We're not talking about evaluating the impact of a single published article or a play you wrote but of your career of research projects that generated impacts.

- If you have been using the tool throughout your career, the ultimate case study can be a synthesis of the case studies you have previously written. However, if you are now at a mature stage in your career you can use the same principles in the tool, but instead of interviewing stakeholders confined to one project, you can interview those who have been with you on your entire professional journey. You can ask them about their recollections of working with you and how those collaborations produced evidence that they used to do their jobs better. Examples could include how your research allowed them to develop more responsive public policies, deliver more effective professional practice, make a better widget or produce artistic presentations to critical acclaim. This can establish your impact track record and will be useful in the event you are applying to funders like the Australian National Health and Medical Research Council (NHMRC) that doesn't ask for a pathway to impact per se but asks you to include a statement on your personal impact track record.

CONCLUSION

Dear Researcher, you might be in the UK and asked to contribute to an impact case study for the next research impact assessment exercise. You may be in Australia and have to write a personal impact statement for an NHMRC grant application. You could be in Canada, needing to collect and communicate the evidence of impact of a career of research for a SSHRC Impact Award nomination. You might be anywhere receiving funding from a health charity and need to demonstrate that your research is making a difference to patients and families. Now you have a tool that will help you collect and communicate the evidence of impact.

Go forth, dear Researcher. You're making an impact. Adapt this tool to your own context and let everyone else know how you are changing the world through your research!

NOTES

1. https://researchimpact.ca/kmb_resource/impact-and-engagement-case-study-guidelines/.
2. https://kidsbrainhealth.ca/index.php/2020/03/27/hand-in-hand-changing-at-risk-kids-trajectories-by-supporting-early-development-2/.
3. http://www.ideas-idees.ca/sites/default/files/2014-10-03-impact-project-draft-report-english-version-final2.pdf.
4. http://rev.oxfordjournals.org/content/early/2012/11/14/reseval.rvs027.full.

5. Phipps, Cummings, Pepler, Craig, and Cardinal (2016).
6. http://bit.ly/1FDJPLm.
7. http://bit.ly/1osEl2W.
8. http://www.ref.ac.uk/.
9. http://www.hefce.ac.uk/pubs/rereports/Year/2015/ana-lysisREFimpact/.
10. http://www.sshrc-crsh.gc.ca/about-au_sujet/publications/KMb_evaluation_2013_e.pdf.

REFERENCES

Adam, P., Ovseiko, P. V., Grant, J., Graham, K. E. A., Boukhris, O. F., Dowd, A.-M., Balling, G. V., Christensen, R. N., Pollitt, A., Taylor, M., Sued, O., Hinrichs-Krapels, S., Solans-Domènech, M., Chorzempa, H., & the International School on Research Impact Assessment (ISRIA). (2018). ISRIA statement: Ten-point guidelines for an effective process of research impact assessment. *Health Research Policy and Systems*, *16*(8), 1–16. https://doi.org/10.1186/s12961-018-0281-5

Cruz Rivera, S., Kyte, D. G., Aiyegbusi, O. L., Keeley, T. J., & Calvert, M. J. (2017). Assessing the impact of healthcare research: A systematic review of methodological frameworks. *PLoS Medicine*, *14*(8), e1002370. https://doi.org/10.1371/journal.pmed.1002370

Greenhalgh, T., Raferty, J., Hanney, S., & Glover, M. (2016). Research impact: A narrative review. *BMC Medicine*, *14*(78), 1–16. https://bmcmedicine.biomedcentral.com/articles/10.1186/s12916-016-0620-8

King's College London and Digital Science. (2015). *The nature, scale and beneficiaries of research impact: An initial analysis of Research Excellence Framework (REF) 2014 impact case studies*. HEFCE. https://www.kcl.ac.uk/policy-institute/research-analysis/nature-scale-beneficiaries-research-impact

MacGregor, S., & Phipps, D. (2020). How a networked approach to building capacity in knowledge mobilization supports research impact. *International Journal of Education Policy & Leadership*, *16*(5). https://journals.sfu.ca/ijepl/index.php/ijepl/issue/view/179

Morton, S. (2015). Progressing research impact assessment: A 'contributions' approach. *Research Evaluation*, *24*(4), 405–419. http://rev.oxfordjournals.org/content/24/4/405

Phipps, D. J., Cummings, J., Pepler, D., Craig, W., & Cardinal, S. (2016). The *Co-produced Pathway to impact* describes knowledge mobilization processes. *Journal of Community Engagement and Scholarship*, *9*(1), 31–40.

Riley, B. L., Kernoghan, A., Stockton, L., Montague, S., Yessis, J., & Willis, C. D. (2018). Using contribution analysis to evaluate the impacts of research on policy: Getting to 'good enough'. *Research Evaluation*, *27*(1), 16–27. https://doi.org/10.1093/reseval/rvx037

Smith, K. E., Bandola-Gill, J., Meer, N., Stewart, E., & Watermeyer, R. (2020). *The impact Agenda*. Policy Press.

Wróblewska, M. N. (2021). Research impact evaluation and academic discourse. *Humanities and Social Sciences Communications*, *8*, 58. https://doi.org/10.1057/s41599-021-00727-8

**Research Impact Canada
(RIC) Impact and Engagement
Case Study Guidelines**

RESEARCH | Turning
IMPACT | research
CANADA | into action

RESEARCH IMPACT CANADA MISSION

We build Canada's capacity to be a leader in creating value from knowledge by developing and sharing best practices, services and tools, and by demonstrating to relevant stakeholders and the public the positive impacts of mobilising knowledge.

RESEARCH IMPACT CANADA VISION

A globally leading network which supports researchers, students and their partners to demonstrate the contribution to and impact of research excellence.

BACKGROUND

The Canadian Federation of Humanities and Social Sciences (CFHSS) released a report (October 2014) titled 'The Impacts of Social Sciences and Humanities Research'.[3] This report acknowledges the challenges but also the importance of demonstrating impacts arising from social sciences and humanities. CFHSS identified five impacts of SSH research including impacts on: scholarship, capacity (training), economy, society and culture, and practice and policy. Similarly the Canadian Academy of Health Sciences developed a health research impact assessment framework that identified how health research can inform decisions in sectors beyond the academy such as in health authorities, industry, government, non-profit organisations and the public.[4]

RIC has a vision consistent with these Canadian examples. RIC supports knowledge brokers and knowledge mobilisation including engaged scholarship, community based research, service learning and public engagement. Collectively these institutional practices help to maximise the social, cultural, health, environmental and economic impacts of academic research.

DEFINITIONS

Research

Impact (see below) may arise as a function of new knowledge created by academic researchers and trainees (students and post-doctoral fellows) as part of university research and learning activities. New knowledge might have been co-created through collaboration with non-academic research partners (see below). New knowledge is often codified through academic dissemination methods as well as in creative works and 'grey literature' including electronic dissemination and social media.

Research Expertise

Impact may also be created by academic researchers and trainees applying their knowledge to an opportunity beyond the academy. When collaborating with non-academic partners, academic expertise is valued equally with non-academic expertise derived from lived experience, community/indigenous knowledge, practice-based knowledge and knowledge from industry and policy partners.

Research Impact

Impact is defined as an effect on, change or benefit to the economy, society, culture, public policy or services, health, the environment or quality of life, beyond academia. Impact includes, but is not limited to, an effect on, change or benefit to:

1. the activity, attitude, awareness, behaviour, capacity, opportunity, performance, policy, practice, process or understanding

2. an audience, beneficiary, community, constituency, organisation or individuals

3. any geographic location whether locally, regionally, nationally or internationally.

Impact includes the reduction or prevention of harm, risk, cost or other negative effects.

Engagement with and dissemination to non-academic audiences is not considered research impact unless that engagement activity is evaluated to establish a change or effect on activities, attitudes and awareness of the non-academic audience. However engagement is a prerequisite for impact so collecting the evidence of engagement may be an early indicator of potential impact.

Exclusions for assessing impact:

1. Impacts on research or the advancement of academic knowledge within the higher education sector are excluded.

2. Impacts on students, teaching or other activities within the university are excluded.

Impact is usually not a report, journal article or other form of knowledge dissemination unless dissemination of that product can be linked to impact as defined above in which case the report isn't the impact, but the report enabled the subsequent impact that is then described in the case study.

Benefits of Research Engagement

As illustrated in the co-produced pathway to impact, benefits accrue to academic and non-academic stakeholders as research progresses towards impact even if it hasn't yet achieved impact on policies, products and/or services.[5] These benefits include engagement with and dissemination to non-academic audiences so long as those non-academic audiences can articulate the benefits accruing as a result of the engagement and/or dissemination.

Non-Academic Research Stakeholder

A non-academic research stakeholder is an individual or organisation that has an interest in the research and its impact. A stakeholder might include individuals with lived experience, a community or government representative, a corporate partner or donor or an organisation that is connected to the subject matter. Stakeholders may or may not contribute materially (cash or in kind contributions) to the research or its translation into impacts. Their contributions might be in the form of input based on lived experience. When possible, the perspectives of diverse stakeholders should be engaged throughout the research process from inception, to design, execution, evaluation and dissemination; however, different non-academic research stakeholders might play discrete roles at different stages of the pathway from research to impact.

USING THIS TOOL

Before using this tool, consider asking the principal investigator for a general overview and history of the project; the impact assessor needs to have a general understanding of the research, the partners/stakeholders and the intended beneficiaries. Often you will hear background that does not come out in response to the first question in the interview guide.

The tool is comprised of three sections: guidelines, semi-structured interview guide and case study template.

1. Guidelines: This tool is informed by the theories of CA and the critical role of non-academic partners in mediating impacts of research.[6–7]

2. Semi-structured Interview Guide

   • After reviewing the guidelines and speaking to the principle investigator, the impact assessor will identify impact stakeholders and arrange separate interviews with each. The semi-structured interview questions are designed as a guide. Interviewing stakeholders will naturally take you down to tangents you didn't expect. Follow those tangents, but come back to the interview guide to ensure all relevant information is collected.

   • As the interview progresses, the impact assessor should ask the interview subject for corroborating evidence in the form of reports, blogs, committee minutes, videos etc. Evidence of impact beyond the academy or benefits arising from engaged research can also be backed up by references to grey literature, programme/policy documentation, press releases and product sales. Reach of a described impact may be documented using social media analytics; however, on their own social media, web-based analytics are measures of dissemination not impact beyond the academy.

3. Case Study Template: The template allows the user to collect the evidence that describes the narrative of the research impact. It is based on the REF (UK, 2014) impact case study template and accompanying guidelines.[8]

   • Using data derived from interviews with stakeholders including researchers, partners and receptors plus corroborating evidence allows the impact assessor to complete the six questions in the RIC case study template. The completed case study template will serve as the unit of assessment for impact. Research on the REF confirmed that the narrative case study is the optimal unit of research impact assessment.[9] Impact assessors may use the completed case study to inform a variety of communication actions including web stories (i.e. blog), newsletter content, video and social media.

   • A complete narrative includes quantitative metrics where possible (clients served, waiting hours saved, commute time reduced, money saved, % increase in performance such as scores on standard tests). No numbers without stories and no stories without numbers.

UNDERSTANDING HOW RESEARCH CAN MAKE AN IMPACT

There are many ways in which research may have underpinned impact or engagement that helped to create benefits, including but not limited to:

- Research and expertise that contributed directly or indi-
  rectly to benefits or an impact. For example, research may
  have informed research in another submitted unit (whether
  in the same or another institution), which in turn led to an
  impact.

- Research embodied in one or more outputs, conducted by
  one or more individuals, teams or groups, within one or
  more submitted units that led to or underpinned an impact.

- Impacts on, for example, public awareness, attitudes,
  understanding or behaviour that arose from engaging the
  public with research. In these cases, the impact assessor
  must show that the engagement activity was, at least in
  part, based on the research/expertise and drew materially
  and distinctly upon it.

- Researchers whose expertise had an impact on others
  through the provision of professional advice or expert tes-
  timony. In such a case, impact assessors must show that the
  researcher's appointment to their advisory role, or the
  specific advice given, was at least in part based on the
  research and drew materially and distinctly upon it.

- Research that led to impact through its deliberate exploitation by the university or through its exploitation by
  others. The submitting university need not have been
  involved in exploiting the research, but must show that its
  research made a distinct and material contribution to the
  impact.

- Research engagement can identify new research questions
  or create new research priorities driven by the needs of end
  users. Students with an engaged research experience might

be hired by an agency or their research partner creating a job for them. Testimonials about the value of the university to community needs might arise from engaged research.

The onus is on impact assessors to provide appropriate evidence within each case study of the particular impact or benefits claimed. Please refer to the practices described by CA (footnote four above) to collect the evidence of impact. SSHRC evaluated their knowledge mobilisation funding programmes in 2013.[10] This evaluation identified that:

- end of grant reports does not contain evidence of impact beyond the academy

- researchers know little about impact of their research/ expertise once it has been taken up by a non-academic research partner or receptor

- evidence of impact is best collected by interviewing non-academic research stakeholders. Interviews may be conducted by research team or by the knowledge mobilisation support service providers or both.

For additional thoughts on collecting the evidence of impact, please see Appendix 3.

USING THE IMPACT ASSESSMENT TEMPLATE FOR ASSESSING ENGAGEMENT (I.E. NOT YET IMPACT)

Not all projects will progress to impact nor do all submitting units have a focus on impact.

1. Which questions to use?

   • The eight questions in the interview guide (see Appendix
     1) can be used at any time in the research to engagement
     to impact process. Early in the research and engagement
     process, only the first few questions might be appro-
     priate; however, all eight are appropriate for gathering
     the evidence of impact.

2. When to ask the questions?

   • As a project progresses from research to engagement to
     impact, questions should be asked of researchers,
     trainees and stakeholders on an annual basis. Each year,
     the previous answers can be reviewed and subsequent
     questions can be asked. This allows the submitting unit
     to monitor the progress of the project.

   • The non-academic stakeholders will inform you when no
     further progress will be made using the research,
     expertise or evidence.

APPENDIX 1: SAMPLE INTERVIEW QUESTIONS (DERIVED FROM FOOTNOTE 8)

RESEARCH IMPACT ASSESSMENT – STAKEHOLDER INTERVIEW GUIDE

To collect the evidence of the impact of your research/
evidence/project, identify stakeholders (researcher, student,
policymaker, practitioner, teacher, clinician, social worker
etc.) and interview the stakeholder using the questions below
as a guide. Adapt these questions to suit your context and
allow them to evolve as the interview evolves.

1. *Context:* (a) History – how did
You Get involved in This project; (b)
Role – what was/Is your role in
your organisation; (c) Inputs: what were the human,
financial, technical resources available; (d) were
These resources adequate for the needs of the
project; (e) Who had control over These resources?

2. *Responsibility:* (a) Activities – beyond the research, what activities
were carried out to address the issues identified by stakeholders (see
#3); (b) Responsibility – what was your responsibility in the project; (c)
Responsibility – how critical was your role to the process; (d) Other – did
you have any other roles in the project?

3. *Awareness/reaction:* (a) Aims: from your perspective, what was the
aim of the project; (b) beliefs – what were your initial beliefs/
perspectives; (c) Reaction – what were your initial reactions to the
project and did these change over the course of the project?

4. *Engagement/involvement:* (a) People Who were the key stakeholders/
partners in the project; (b) How – how were you engaged; (c) Gaps –
were there any challenges in this engagement; (d) Others – were there
any stakeholders/partners that weren't engaged; (e) Others – what
might have been accomplished if they had been engaged?

5. *Capacity/knowledge/skills:* (a) What capacity/skills did you (and other
stakeholders/participants) have for using/applying/learning from/
disseminating this research; (b) did you have the resources to do so?

6. *Changes:* (a) For you – what happened for you/your organisation as a
result of the project; (b) More broadly – what changed for your
organization/sector and how do you know/what is the evidence for the
change; (c) Unanticipated – what happened in the project that you
didn't anticipate?

7. *Impact:* (a) Change What longer term change has resulted/is resulting from the project for you/your organisation/sector; (b) Attribution – what other factors were/are also influencing the long term impact (social, political, economic, environmental)

8. *Next Steps:* (a) Current state – are you still engaged in the project; (b) Where to from here – what would you like to see happen next?

APPENDIX 2: ASSESSMENT TEMPLATES

A. RESEARCH IMPACT ASSESSMENT TEMPLATE

You are asked to describe the impact of your research/evidence/project.

Once you have interviewed the non-academic stakeholder (Interview Guide), complete the template below describing the impact and/or engagement, the research/expertise that underpins the impact and cite the evidence of the impact. Adapt these sections to suit your context.

1. *Title of Case Study*

2. *Summary of the impact:* briefly describe the impact of the research beyond the academic research

3. *Contribution of research and/or expertise:* Describe the academic and non-academic research and/or expertise, evidence or project that underpins the impact

4. *References to the research and/or expertise:* Maximum of six references from the academic or 'grey' literature that describe the underlying research and/or expertise described in #3 above

5. *Details of the impact:* Describe in detail the nature, extent, reach, sustainability, stakeholders and beneficiaries of the impact summarised in #2 above

6. *Sources to corroborate the impact:* How do you know this impact occurred – cite data sources, interviews with stakeholders and researchers, data from the implementation of a new policy, product or service.

7. *Role of knowledge mobilisation contributing to the impact:* Describe the activities undertaken by the research impact practitioners (researchers, students, partners, knowledge brokers, etc).

APPENDIX 3: SOME REFLECTIONS ON COLLECTING THE EVIDENCE OF IMPACT

Stephen Kemp.
8 June 2018

GUIDANCE ON TESTIMONIALS AND STATEMENTS TO CORROBORATE IMPACT

https://blogs.lse.ac.uk/impactofsocialsciences/2018/06/08/
guidance-on-testimonials-and-statements-to-corroborate-
impact/

The REF impact assessment requires impact case studies to include evidence of impact. This evidence can take many forms, quantitative or qualitative. Statements from research users, stakeholders and beneficiaries can be a powerful form of qualitative evidence, as seen in REF 2014.

WHAT TO INCLUDE

In general, statements should:

1. Be written on the external organisation's headed paper (or a suitably professional-looking email).

2. Be signed by someone at an appropriate level. This will vary by case study but considerations should include seniority vs connection to the research (e.g. should the statement come from your direct contact, the person with responsibility for the area or the head of the organisation?), maturity of relationship, reputation and conflicts of interest.

3. Name the researcher and refer to the research (could be in descriptive terms, citation of a research output, name of research programme – whatever comes across as most fitting).

4. Describe how the organisation 'found' the research/ researcher.

5. Describe how it fits with the organisation's activities, strategy, needs, challenges, opportunities and other drivers.

6. Describe how the research/knowledge/skills were put into action or used – e.g. did the organisation work with the academic (maybe through commissioned research, consultancy, knowledge transfer grant, advisory work, other joint activities), did they use the research in their decision-making, did they train their staff according to the research?

7. Describe what happened as a result of using the research/ knowledge/skills or working with the researcher – e.g. did they produce guidelines for practice, were they better informed in making strategic decisions, was their service provision directly improved?

8. Describe the resulting impact of this work – what was the benefit of using the research/knowledge or working with the researcher? Include quantitative or qualitative indicators to show the impact – i.e. how they know it was beneficial. They could also say where they'd be if they *hadn't* used the research. This is the most important part of the statement as its where the impact is really articulated (and any quantitative/qualitative evidence the organisation provides can be quoted in the case study and woven into the narrative).

9. Say something about the future – what's next in this line of work? Do they foresee continued and growing benefits? Will they work with the researcher again? Will they be more open to using academic research in the future? Maybe they'll change the way they operate as a result of the impactful piece of work.

HOW TO GATHER TESTIMONIALS

The first (and by far the best) option is to put the above list into your own words (so it doesn't sound so much like a checklist) and use this to prompt a statement from your partner. You could either put it in writing and let them respond accordingly or you could use this as the basis of a conversation/interview. The beauty of the latter approach is that you can explore and clarify and it may uncover other relevant information.

Secondly, you could use the above list as a checklist/questionnaire. I wouldn't recommend this approach. It may save time but you are unlikely to get the richness or authenticity of a more personal/tailored interaction. It won't strengthen your relationship with the organisation, and it may even damage it.

Finally, in some cases, it may be necessary to essentially write the statement yourself and hand it over to the partner to sign. This is not recommended as you lose the authentic voice and you may miss some aspect of what made the work so valuable (including possibly some extra information the partners would have included if they'd had to write it themselves). On top of this there is a very real risk that if the academic writes a number of such letters for different partners to sign, they could all end up looking fundamentally the same which undermines the credibility of the messages. Consider how you'd view this as an assessor...

OTHER CONSIDERATIONS

- Make sure the person giving the statement knows what it is for and has the authority to give it.

- Observe the relevant data management and ethics policies as you gather, hold and use this information.

- In REF 2014, some organisations were overwhelmed with requests for testimonials to the point where relationships were affected and in some cases, they simply refused to provide testimonials. This is where strong relationships really count, so focus on lasting, rather than superficial, interactions with stakeholders and partners.

- Some organisations will be concerned about confidentiality. Although we don't currently know how this will work for impact case studies and evidence in REF 2021, there were provisions for this in REF 2014, so we can expect similar in REF 2021.

- Don't wait to get testimonials. The details, nature and value of impacts may become dull with time so jump on them while they're fresh. Plus you never know where people will be in a couple of years.

The link to the tool in English is https://researchimpact.ca/kmb_resource/impact-and-engagement-case-study-guidelines/

The link to the tool in French is https://researchimpact.ca/fr/kmb_resource/impact-and-engagement-case-study-guidelines/

8

THE LONG VIEW: BUILDING AN IMPACT PLAN ON YOUR TERMS

Faith Welch

ABSTRACT

The penultimate chapter pulls together pieces of the previous eight chapters to support you in building a career-level impact plan. While the other chapters are a mix of foundational knowledge and practical approaches, this chapter is more philosophical in nature and intended to motivate the reader to bring their impact journey to life. You are encouraged to reflect on your own journey and consider what steps you might take to achieve a career that is consistent with your values and own belief in the importance of the work you do. Contributions from impactful researchers from the University of Auckland help to illustrate how diverse career pathways can be, emphasising there is no one-size-fits-all approach and that career-level impact plans need to consider personal motives and values, intersectionality, as well as disciplinary, institutional, national and international contexts. Plans need to focus on identifying opportunities to hone impact skills, finding people who can be part of your broader impact support team and working out how to strategically balance the teaching, research and service expectations placed on you as an academic. Throughout this chapter, questions prompt you to start building your own understanding of impact in the context of your career or to strategically reflect on your impact journey up to now.

Keywords: Impact plan; career plan; career pathways; strategy; careers; research impact; higher education

INTRODUCTION

Whilst most of this book has been a mix of foundational knowledge and practical approaches, this chapter is more philosophical in nature and intended to motivate you to bring your impact journey to life. It's important to take time and reflect on where you have been, where you would like to go and what steps you might take to achieve a career that is consistent with your values and own belief in the importance of the work you do.

To help you reflect on your own career path, and to illustrate how diverse these journeys can be, a series of in-depth interviews were conducted with academics from the University of Auckland who have had significant impact in some key areas.

Associate Professor Siouxsie Wiles, a microbiologist who was awarded the accolade of New Zealander of the Year (2021) for her clear research communication throughout the COVID-19 pandemic.

Dr Sereana Naepi, a social scientist who engages with Māori and Pacific communities to improve equity within higher education.

Professor Cather Simpson, a medical scientist turned chemist turned physicist turned entrepreneur solving complex industry challenges with sustainability and health benefits.

Professor James Russell, a conservation biologist working with Predator Free New Zealand to protect endemic species.

Each of these academics brings unique perspectives to why and how they have had impactful careers, emphasising that there is no one-size-fits-all approach and that career-level impact plans need to consider personal motives and values, intersectionality, as well as disciplinary, institutional, national and international contexts.

Plans need to focus on identifying opportunities to hone impact skills, finding people who can be part of your broader impact support team and working out how to strategically balance the teaching, research and service expectations placed on you as an academic.

Throughout this chapter, questions prompt you to start building your own understanding of impact in the context of your career, or to strategically reflect on your impact journey up to now. While much is to be gained by reading through this chapter, its usefulness will be deepened if you approach it like a workshop, with opportunities to reflect and plan throughout. Grab a pencil and paper and read on...

WHAT DRIVES YOU TO BE A RESEARCHER?

I ask this question as an ice-breaker at nearly every single training session I run to show my participants that the fundamental nature of a researcher is to seek change. When I ask 'what drives or motivates your research?', the answers I hear most often are along the lines of a combination of curiosity, problem-solving, making a difference and contributing to making the world a better place. Ask yourself this question, and try and go deeper than a surface answer. Don't answer it how you would for a funder; answer it as though you were writing it in your eulogy.

The researchers I interviewed agreed; their love for their specific research area was curiosity driven and the impact lens they put over it was driven by their individual values. James discussed with me his love of birds as a child: Growing up I wanted to work in sustainability – specifically bird conservation. That led me to take the degrees I did, ask the questions I do, and seek to create the change I want to see.

Siouxsie takes a bigger picture approach to her impact. Whilst the nature of her research is often quite fundamental, finding anti-microbials from fungi, she said she is driven to communicate as she 'want[s] to be part of making this country or this world the kind of place I want to live'. Similarly, Sereana's career pathway was influenced by her earlier experiences: 'I was angry at how slow the academic system was to support Māori and Pacific students', she said, 'so I did my masters in how to better support Māori and Pacific student success'.

ASK YOURSELF: What drives you to be a researcher? What attracted you to this career path in the first place, and what sustains you? What are things you wish you could change?

WHAT DOES IMPACT MEAN TO YOU?

It is not just your motives and drivers that will shape your impact journey. It is your own personal vision of *what impact is* – this will be key to unlocking your goals. Unless bound by impact definitions from funders or national assessments (see chapter 1), our individual definitions of impact do not need to be restricted. What it means to be an impactful academic to one person will mean something different to the next, and you need to work out what this means to you.

Siouxsie described her impact as 'the intersection between my specialist knowledge which comes from my research and teaching, and the desire to be a better communicator, which I have worked on for ten years. This has resulted in very clear impact: helping people to understand the pandemic'. Whereas Cather sees most of her impact in the people she teaches and trains: 'If Engender [one of her spin-out companies] fails tomorrow, we would still make a huge impact as we have had 30 or 40 people come through the company who can create new ideas, solve problems and have further impact'. For Sereana, impact is part of her culture and community involvement in research is the traditional way of doing things. She said, 'the research impact space is exciting as it validates what Māori and Pacific researchers have done for a long time'. Whilst these responses are all quite different, they are linked by their impact work requiring them to actively engage with others and impact being on the people they work with.

ASK YOURSELF: What does impact mean to you? What difference do you want to make? What positive changes do you most want to contribute to? Who do you want to have impact with?

DISCOVERING YOUR INSTITUTIONAL, NATIONAL AND GEOPOLITICAL CONTEXT

As the case studies show, impact journeys can differ vastly within a single research institution. Each interviewee has their own highly individual perspective of impact, and there will be infinite other perspectives and experiences that are valid. Discipline, impact goal, culture, intersectionality and much more contribute to the shape of your impact career plan. Our institutional, national and geopolitical contexts just add another layer of complexity, and you need to be aware of how you can leverage your context to support your impact journey.

Institutional context. Work by Drs Julie Bayley and David Phipps has led to us referring to how impact-healthy an institution is.[1] This accounts for the institution's commitment to impact through strategy and resource; the internal connectivity of individuals and teams to help drive impact; how clearly impact is understood within the institution; the level of impact competencies (in terms of both development opportunities and specialists); and the extent and quality of engagement with non-academics to co-design and co-produce impactful research. The healthier your institution, the easier it will be to drive impact of your own research. But even if your institution is at the beginning of its impact journey, it doesn't necessarily mean your impact will be curtailed. You'll need to think more creatively about how you drive the impact of your work, how you advocate for research impact internally, where you find specialist support and what you will need to bring your impact plan to life. If you are struggling with where to start, perhaps start a network inviting like-minded academics to discuss impact issues or look outside of the institution for resources.

ASK YOURSELF: Is my institution committed to supporting impact? Is there an institutional impact strategy? Are there associated resources? What are the avenues for advocating for research impact within my institution?

National Context. The national context will drive the institutional context, so consider these aspects concurrently. If you live in a country with national assessment of research impact (see chapter 1), then the associated definitions and indicators of success are likely to drive what your institution sees as important in terms of impact. If that national impact assessment is linked to funding, then it can be expected for your institution to have additional resources, infrastructure and experts to help mobilise knowledge, support engagement and ultimately accelerate your impact. However, these resources may potentially be limited by the scope of the assessment system and not support certain forms of impact that don't 'count'. Since the introduction of impact assessment in the UK's Research Excellence Framework (REF) 2014, there has been a proliferation of impact funds to accelerate impact activity and professional roles to support mobilisation of knowledge and capture of impact evidence: some are generic and some are highly REF-specific. And there are similar assessments across the world which are quickly driving an increase in impact resourcing in their own national research ecosystems such as Engagement and Impact Assessment in Australia and the Research Assessment Exercise in Hong Kong.

There is currently no mandatory impact assessment as part of New Zealand's national assessment of research excellence, the Performance Based Research Fund, and yet impactful research is still generated. In the New Zealand context, impact is being driven at many different levels; individual members of the research ecosystem including funders, research institutions and individual research groups are developing their own impact missions which are collectively driving change. The implementation of impact resourcing, infrastructure and recognition in a mission-driven system is slower than in an assessment-driven system, but it is perhaps more inclusive and could lead to more sustainable change. Regardless of its origins, there is likely some form of impact agenda wherever you are geographically located.

ASK YOURSELF: Is there a national assessment of research impact? Do key players in the national research ecosystem have impact strategies or missions? Which of these key players influence my research?

Geopolitical context. With only five million people, New Zealand is a relatively small country whose size can really help enable impact. James said: 'In a small country it forces us to interact with people who aren't just academics'. Siouxsie added, 'what's extraordinary, or an advantage around our size as a country, is the degree of separation between you and the Director General of Health, or you and the government's science advisors'. In short, it can be easier to engage with people who are key to enabling impact. In contrast, however, living on a small set of islands at the end of the earth can be quite a hindrance if your research and its impact are more internationally focused. It forces researchers to think creatively about how to connect their research with stakeholders across the globe, by utilising videoconferencing technology, being highly flexible with work hours to connect on different time zones, and ruthlessly strategic about who and where to travel to.

Another thing that enabled Siouxsie to have impact was the New Zealand government's willingness to listen to the science.

At the start of the pandemic in 2020, the research centre she works with proactively approached the government to provide scientific advice, which was well received. But this simple and direct approach to engaging the science with policy has been embraced by governments overseas to varying degrees and, in some countries, with minimal success. Pandemic aside, the political party in power, the length of term in Parliament, political agendas and research investment strategies can all affect your ability to have impact.

ASK YOURSELF: How does your geopolitical situation help and/or hinder your impact goals?

IDENTIFYING THE SKILLS YOU NEED TO DEVELOP

Traditionally, researchers have been trained to specialise and focus on a narrow field of research, becoming experts in the intricacies of a specific research area, often to the exclusion of other disciplines and non-academic perspectives. However, to address the greatest challenges and generate an impact on the world, it may be necessary to expand your skill horizons.

James described the potential pitfalls of academic culture and promotion criteria which can, in extreme cases, sway academics away from their original reasons for becoming researchers. '[Academia can] take highly intelligent people and get them distracted and perverted on the games of academic publishing instead of doing something that makes a difference'. He advocates for having the flexibility to retrain; 'after doing natural sciences I picked up a load of social science and soon I'll do something else. I'm looking at disease now'. This has enabled James to collaborate more effectively across disciplines, access funding that was previously unavailable to him and drive broader impact of his research.

Cather had a similar story to tell. She started her academic career in the US and, before moving to New Zealand, had not done any commercialisation. Fast-forward a few years and her spin-out company was acquired – she is currently their Chief Scientific Officer. She explained, 'I took [the role] as it was an opportunity to take something that showed a lot of promise and try to get it to be a product, something I had never done before! It was an exciting learning opportunity'. Cather is now deciding whether she will return to the University or continue working in industry. Whilst she has many considerations to make, she counts herself lucky to have had a successful academic career without necessarily following a traditional path; 'I'm at an interesting juncture where I get to decide what impact I get to have next'.

What these stories tell us is that a successful and impactful academic career is not static. Consider the impact you would like to make and the skills that might help you along the way. These may be in different research areas, or they may be different impact competencies. There are several useful articles (Bayley et al., 2018; Nicholson & Howard, 2018) that describe the skills required to enable research impact. Pick those that you are interested in developing and that align with your values, but don't try to be a superacademic! You can, and very likely should, collaborate with researchers in complementary disciplines, work with experts that can help mobilise the knowledge, engage artists that can bring your communication to life, leverage cultural navigators to support engagement and work with commercialisation specialists to help you navigate the intellectual property (IP) landscape.

Sereana and the team she collaborates with often seek out artists to bring their research messages to life. She explained; 'we work with artists a lot now. Because [the members of the transdisciplinary research team] all think about things differently, we think of different ways to communicate our ideas'.

But her and her team have had to think creatively about funding this type of expert, as funds in New Zealand are limited for this type of public engagement. She said, 'we don't have money for it. But I'm already thinking about how I can use my Early Career Research Excellence Award to fund her'.

ASK YOURSELF: What broader skills would you like to develop? What impact competencies are important in driving your research impact? Where might you engage with experts?

FINDING YOUR PEOPLE

Impact is a team sport, but this often conflicts with how we are trained as individual researchers. Graduate research degrees and postdoctoral fellowships can be a very solitary experience and can perpetuate working solo. As your career progresses, you may continue to conduct research individually to understand a problem, tackle a challenge, or fill a knowledge gap. However, increasingly there is a global understanding that whilst disciplinary knowledge is a vital foundation, interdisciplinary or even transdisciplinary research is required to address complex societal challenges (OECD, 2020); to achieve impact you will likely need to work with many people. There are those with different disciplinary knowledge who can bring new ontologies, methodologies and perspectives to your research, people with similar values who can provide a support network, individuals with similar impact goals who can provide mentorship and those that bring specialist expertise to help mobilise knowledge or engage with stakeholders. Consider who you need in your impact team and where you are going to find your people.

Cather built a reputation for having a team known as 'the lab that solved problems'. She explained, 'I worked really hard to build teams that could deliver on what we promised.' In the case of her company Engender Technologies Limited, a spin-out that has developed a technology to separate X- and Y-bearing bull sperm cells, she said 'I'm not a sperm sorting person, and a lot of the stuff we use to sort semen I've never used before! But we pull together a team, everyone is focused on a project, and bringing the expertise you need and hope-fully something really good comes out of it'.

Siouxsie described how important it was to have a support team around her of like-minded individuals, with similar values and similar goals. She connected with colleagues in her research centre because the centre was developed with, 'how we want researchers to be and research to be done', as its central focus. The centre brings in people from different dis-ciplines, cultures and with different lived experiences and places an equity lens on the research. She said, 'this has allowed the kind of research the centre does to have incredible impact'.

ASK YOURSELF: Who do you need in your impact team? Who could provide a new perspective to your research? Who could provide mentorship to meet your impact goals? Where is your support network?

BALANCING THE EXPECTATIONS PLACED ON YOU AS AN ACADEMIC

Reflecting an increased emphasis on impact, University pro-motion criteria and academic standards are in flux globally. For example, Utrecht University launched their new Recog-nition and Rewards model in 2021, abandoning journal impact factors and embracing open research and societal impact.[2] However, most research institutions are still firmly embedded with traditional metrics of success such as publications and funding, and impact is often unrecognised and unrewarded. Generating impact through strategic engagement can also take considerable time and effort, taking you away from the things that your employer may deem more important (e.g. publishing in high-impact journals, taking on high teaching loads). The researchers interviewed had different approaches to balancing the teaching, research and service expectations placed on them.

Cather said, 'I'm pretty proactive about getting that balance. I decided very early on in my career I was going to live my values. So, I volunteer for service jobs that are in line with my values, including women in leadership, […] compassionate consideration, academic integrity. Anything I can do to support underrepresented groups to succeed. I teach because I love it and it is where I have the most amount of impact and I derive a lot of pleasure from helping other people figure out how they're going to succeed with their own goals. And the science is the same. I do what I value and that means I don't agonise'. For Cather, her values come first and the impact follows…..

Siouxsie has struggled to find balance. Whilst there is high demand for her clear, articulate and thoughtful communication, she is still tackling a full-time academic role. She has sought support to lessen her teaching load and engages in crowdfunding to cover some of her research projects, but continues to teach, supervise students and apply for funding to support future research.

Sereana describes herself as being 'ruthlessly strategic'. With a young family at home, it is a priority to switch off in the evening. So she reminds us that impact is often a collective piece and the different collectives she works with know each other's priorities and work to collectively engage in impact.

ASK YOURSELF: Do your values align with your teaching, research and service workloads? Can you be more strategic with your work-life balance? What could you do to relieve pressure in one area to allow you to focus on impact?

IN CONCLUSION...WHAT ARE YOUR IMPACT STRENGTHS?

Having read through this chapter and considered the prompts throughout, you should start to have an idea of what your personal impact trajectory across the career span may look like. But don't stop here. I challenge you to reach out to the impactful academics around you, take them for a well-earned coffee or a long walk and learn from their experiences.

ASK YOURSELF: What situations do you thrive in? What role do you see yourself having in driving impact? What are your personal strengths for creating impact?

But don't forget to think about what *your* impact strengths are. Siouxsie is an extroverted confident communicator, comfortable with her role in the spotlight; Sereana is naturally collaborative, leaning on her personal drivers to push for change; Cather and James are both very willing to learn new things and use their curiosity to push themselves outside of their comfort zones. You don't have to be exactly like another impactful researcher; there is a space and pathway to impact for everyone that can work to your own strengths. There is only one you, so what impact can you bring about that no one else can?

NOTES

1. https://www.emeraldpublishing.com/wordpress/wp-content/uploads/Emerald-Resources-Institutional-Healthcheck-Workbook.pdf.
2. https://www.uu.nl/en/research/open-science/tracks/recognition-and-rewards.

REFERENCES

Bayley, J. E., Phipps, D., Batac, M., & Stevens, E. (2018). Development of a framework for knowledge mobilisation and impact competencies. *Evidence and Policy: A Journal of Research, Debate and Practice*, *14*(4), 725–738. https://doi.org/10.1332/174426417X14945838375124

Nicholson, J., & Howard, K. (2018). A study of core competencies for supporting roles in engagement and impact assessment in Australia. *Journal of the Australian Library and Information Association*, *67*(2), 131–146. https://doi.org/10.1080/24750158.2018.1473907

OECD. (2020). *Addressing societal challenges using transdisciplinary research. OECD science, technology and industry policy papers, No. 88*. OECD Publishing. https://doi.org/10.1787/0ca0ca45-en

9

TOWARDS THE IMPACTFUL ACADEMIC: THE IMPACTFUL RESEARCHER'S SETTINGS FOR SUCCESS

Wade Kelly

ABSTRACT

This final chapter reviews the key themes of the previous chapters to paint a picture of what it is to be an impactful academic. The reader is prompted to build strategies into their workflow and lives to ensure that impact remains a priority considering the many competing requirements in their roles. The chapter provides strategies for keeping impact on track by engaging both internal and external networks. As government priorities change, higher education will continue to morph and evolve. The impactful academic builds skills throughout their career span, and these skills increase resiliency in the face of a rapidly changing higher education sector; skills that are increasingly critical to career success. The chapter takes stock of skill development related to academic identity and impact goals and encourages readers to continue their impact journey through reflective practice.

Keywords: Research impact; early career research; REF; research engagement; higher education; professional development; academia; career development; tenure; promotion; PhD student

This final chapter reviews the key themes of the previous chapters to paint a picture of what it is to be an impactful academic. The reader is prompted to build strategies into their workflow and lives to ensure that impact remains a priority considering the many competing requirements in their roles. The chapter provides strategies for keeping impact on track by engaging both internal and external networks. As government priorities change, higher education will continue to morph and evolve. The impactful academic builds skills throughout their career span, and these skills increase resiliency in the face of a rapidly changing higher education sector; skills that are increasingly critical to career success. The chapter takes stock of skill development related to academic identity and impact goals and encourages readers to continue their impact journey through reflective practice.

The previous chapters provided various approaches to being and becoming an impactful academic. The authors furnished reflective prompts, helpful metaphors, easy-to-apply frameworks and salient examples to illustrate the complexity of the impact space and ways to navigate it. While everyone will be at different stages in their impact journey, it is hoped that even established impactful academics will find space to reflect on their research impact practice critically. In this chapter, I discuss how to keep the wheels in motion on your journey to becoming an impactful academic.

IN THE EARLY DAYS

When working with PhD students, I often encourage them to focus on the engagement processes rather than the endpoint of impact. Some PhD projects may produce impact(s), but that is a lofty goal. Most PhD programmes do not focus on engagement or impact skills. Instead, the PhD focuses on developing research skills. However, if you can sharpen your ability to do engagement work during the period of your PhD, you will effectively set yourself on an impact trajectory.

Over nine years, I ran Nerd Nite (three 20-minute nerdy talks in a bar) in three cities. I worked with dozens of academics across career stages, assisting them in putting their presentations together. Over the years, I found that senior academics often had more difficulty presenting in that format than early career researchers. Senior researchers had a lifetime of experience presenting to largely homogeneous groups, generally other researchers in the same or adjacent fields. They had learnt a way of presenting that served them well in their careers. Presenting complex topics to a room full of people with drinks in their hands was often not something they were prepared for or had experience doing. The impact agenda increasingly requires academics to possess knowledge translation skills for a wide range of audiences.

I encourage PhD students, candidates and their supervisors to expose themselves and their work to various audiences. Learning to be conversant in non-academic lingo is crucial to working with industry partners, community groups, government, and non-governmental organisations (NGOs). You can wade into the oral public dissemination waters in venues like Nerd Nite, your local Rotary Club, the radio station and podcasts. They are relatively low risk but can be substantial learning opportunities.

These skills are essential building blocks, but it is never too late. Two years after working with a mid-career academic on a five-minute talk for a public event, she contacted me. She told me that the hour we spent crafting that pitch had changed her career. For years, she was telling the wrong story to funders. The funds started rolling in when she focused on the human story and her research's potential to change lives. Doing the five-minute talk forced her to think about the audience differently.

Learning how to pitch yourself – for example, to a radio producer – to get in front of an audience is a skill. Learning how to talk about the importance of the work to various audiences is another critical skill. If you can do a Three Minute Thesis (3MT) or compete in a pitch session, do it. If you can begin to build these skills during your PhD, you will be a step ahead of many academics.

I challenge students to generate an engagement plan for the PhD duration. What service activities for both presenting and writing can you embed in your PhD experience over the time of the programme? What are professional development opportunities offered elsewhere if coursework does not address required skills? If being an impactful academic is a career aspiration, start with engagement.

CONTINUE TO DEVELOP

To establish an impact pathway, I asked a physiotherapist researcher how physiotherapists learn about new advances in the field. I was a little shocked because he did not know. His whole focus had been on publishing in academic venues. His homework was to conduct a stakeholder analysis (drawing on Mark Reed's work) of who might be interested in his work, locally, nationally and internationally and to rate the level of influence he might have with each stakeholder.[1]

He took the task seriously and talked with academic and professional colleagues to complete the analysis. He came back with an impressive plan. He later told me that it opened his world up and expanded his thinking. He investigated how practice guidelines are generated, who sets the curriculum for trainees and where physios received upgrade training. He also went beyond physiotherapists; he realised that local sporting clubs, competitive national teams, dancers and even acrobats would likely be interested in his findings.

He went on this journey because he kept hearing people talk about impact and decided he should better learn more. He understood he had a knowledge deficit and took steps to develop himself. He is now well on his way as an impactful academic.

Like the example above, I encourage those with professions associated with their discipline (e.g. nursing, education, engineering) to identify opportunities to talk with practitioners – keep one foot in that world. I urge them to stay abreast of the professional association communications channels. For example, if you are an education scholar intended to research schools, knowing how teachers and administrators learn about pedagogical research is crucial; it might be through a union newsletter, a professional association magazine, a school district Facebook group, etc. Learning to write in that genre is another skill (see chapter 6, knowledge mobilisation) and should be part of your research output plan.

Keep developing your impact capability by connecting to and remaining connected to various communities. If you are a fundamental biomedical researcher, find ways to attend industry events. Learn how industry people talk about research and researchers. Do not just tell them what you are working on. Instead, find out what problems they have and what they focus on solving. Consider what capabilities you have that could benefit their organisations. Regardless of whether you are a historian or an astrophysicist, the impact conversation should be one of reciprocity and shared goals.

FIND YOUR PEOPLE

Chapters two and three are all about finding your people within your institution and beyond. As impact is an emerging field, there is plenty to share when you have a network around you. One of the great benefits of doing interdisciplinary workshops is getting new perspectives on your research activities. The molecular biologist may question an established norm in sociology. Having to defend engagement and impact choices can bring new perspectives. Justifying the 'way' creates an opportunity for growth. Impact is new territory for most people, so having colleagues and community partners ask 'why' can dramatically clarify goals.

By way of example, as a research output, a global health research team had developed a robust educational website with videos, modules and lesson plans. It was to be made freely available, and the research team had developed a dissemination strategy. Another researcher in the room asked how they would track who was downloading the materials, and blank stares were returned. The principal researcher and the team were focused on generating impact with outputs of their research but not on collecting evidence of that impact. The suggestion was to collect email addresses so that users could later be contacted and surveyed about whether the materials were being adopted. Having people in your network that can critique your impact planning, brainstorm and provide solutions will strengthen your impact practice.

Sometimes the 'why' or 'why not' requires an outside perspective. Building a community of impactful academics and professional impact-focused staff who can provide this lens for you is helpful in the short term and across the career span. Increasingly, universities have impact communities of practice. If you can join one, do. If there is not one, consider starting one.

CELEBRATE

The impact consultation has lasted over an hour, and we were winding down. We had talked about stakeholders and relationship building. We had discussed research outputs and future planning. As I was walking out of her office, she stopped me and said, 'Quick question, if my research was the basis for a law, would that be impact?' I sat back down.

Sometimes so many things happen so quickly that we forget to take time to celebrate or tell others. In some areas, tall poppy syndrome might also be a factor. I asked the researcher if this was embargoed; it was not. I queried if they had talked to the media unit about it; they had not. They had generated impact through their social research in federal law and did not think to shout it from the rooftops.

The impactful academic shares their successes, not in the service of bragging but in the service of the research. The research to change continuum is tenuous in many situations, but it is worth documenting and discussing when the research contribution to change is clear. Pop it on Twitter and

LinkedIn, sure. But also make sure that it has a place on your CV. When giving academic presentations, talk explicitly about your impact goals and successes. When giving community or stakeholder presentations, ditch the academic presentation altogether. Focus on the impact or intended impacts. Far too often, I see academics provide too much information about methods and run out of time or forget the 'so what' altogether. Finally, and this one is a big one for me, ensure that your bio speaks of your scholarly accomplishments *and* your generated impacts.

Let others know that having your research be adopted and applied is valued – that impact is significant to you. Include impact in your annual reviews, if you can. If you are going for tenure, the impacts you have generated should be reported. Include engagement and impact activities on your website. And be an impact champion at your institution. Regardless of career stage, impact champions are needed.

MAKE TIME FOR IMPACT

Keeping impact on track is not an easy task. Impacts can occur years after research projects have been completed. It is easy to lose track of impact and your impact goals with the grind of teaching, service responsibilities and the relentless pressure to attract more funding and produce high-quality research outputs in top-tier venues. It is easy for impact to fall by the wayside, especially in areas where funding for impact (e.g. grants to mobilise positive research findings) does not exist, where support is limited or where the research impact culture is weak.

I offer academics a few suggestions to keep impact on track and in motion. Embedding an impact plan into your 3–5-year research plan is a good start. This is a document you should revisit every six to 12 months. Include your impact goals and the engagement activities you have planned to achieve them in it. Upon review, rate your progress, modify it and, if possible, talk it through with someone outside your department.

Put a re-occurring item in your calendar, perhaps a half day every four months, to keep in touch with former stakeholders (e.g. project partners). It is incredible how often researchers hear about impacts within organisations and industries because they picked up the phone or sent a friendly note.

For research leaders, including impact as a standing item for research committee meetings communicates the value of impact within the organisation. I have worked with several research centres that have done this, and the types of conversations generated, including the gaps in knowledge, quickly change the culture to one that values impact.

WHAT IS THE IMPACTFUL ACADEMIC?

Much of the advice in the previous chapters can be applied in the short term to grants, impact statements, job applications and promotions, but impact does not have a quick turnaround. The knowledge and skills discussed in this book require revising, honing, refreshing, questioning and reflecting. The impactful academic is a perpetual work in progress.

Academia is one of the very few career paths with no predetermined trajectory. Impact creates new ways of positioning activities within your career that align with your epistemological beliefs about the value of knowledge, who holds it, and how it is adopted and used. In chapter one, I said there is no one right way to be an academic. There is also no one right way to be *an impactful academic*. The authors of this book have provided many of the tools needed, but only you can decide what that will look like for you to be an impactful academic.

NOTE

1. https://www.fasttrackimpact.com/post/2019/03/11/how-to-do-stakeholder-analysis.

INDEX